Using ICT in Foundation Stage Teaching

With love to Katie and Sue, Simon and Rachel and our families.
And in memory of Neil Smith – a wonderful colleague and teacher educator.

Using ICT in Foundation Stage Teaching

Tony Poulter and Jo Basford

First published in 2003 by Learning Matters Ltd.

British Library Cataloguing in Publication Data
A CIP record for this book is available from the British Library.

ISBN 1 903300 75 4

Cover design by Topics – The Creative Partnership
Text design by Code 5 Design Associates Ltd
Project management by Deer Park Productions
Typeset by PDQ Typesetting
Printed and bound in Great Britain by Bell & Bain Ltd, Glasgow

Learning Matters Ltd
33 Southernhay East
Exeter EX1 1NX
01392 215560
info@learningmatters.co.uk
www.learningmatters.co.uk

Contents

Introduction

This book has been written specifically for trainee teachers, both undergraduate and postgraduate, who are looking to work with children in the Foundation Stage. It will also help them to address the following standards in *Qualifying to Teach* (DfES/TTA, 2002):

> ***2. Knowledge and Understanding***
> *Those awarded Qualified Teacher Status must demonstrate:*
>
> ***2.5*** *They know how to use ICT effectively, both to teach their subject and to support their wider professional role.*
>
> ***3. Teaching***
> *Those awarded Qualified Teacher Status must demonstrate:*
>
> ***3.3.10*** *They use ICT effectively in their teaching.*

It may well be helpful in meeting the requirements of 2.1a and 3.3.2a, which refer to knowing, understanding and teaching Foundation Stage children in all six areas of learning outlined in *Curriculum Guidance for the Foundation Stage* (QCA/DfEE, 2000) and, for Reception children, with the objectives in the National Literacy and Numeracy Strategy frameworks.

The book could also prove useful to newly qualified teachers and those more experienced practitioners who have not yet got to grips with the demands of information and communication technology (ICT) in Foundation Stage teaching.

The book focuses on how ICT can enhance teaching and learning in all six areas of learning, namely:

- Personal, Social and Emotional Development;
- Communication, Language and Literacy;
- Mathematical Development;
- Knowledge and Understanding of the World;
- Physical Development;
- Creative Development.

Chapter 1 sets the scene by looking at the place of ICT in the curriculum and, more importantly, its place in the Foundation Stage curriculum. We discuss the impact of ICT on learning, the arguments for, and against, its use and the barriers to ICT reaching its full potential in the Early Years setting. We discuss some strategies for good practice and the ICT tools that might be utilised in *all* six areas of learning. Chapter 2 offers you an opportunity to carry out a self-evaluation of needs with regard to ICT skills for teaching in the Foundation Stage, ICT skills for professional purposes, practice with regard to the Early Learning Goal for ICT and other Early Learning Goals. Chapter 3 looks at planning, assessment, management and organisational issues. Chapters 4–9 suggest topics that might be used to teach ICT through the areas of learning over the period of a school year. After some initial discussion a medium-term and a short-term plan are given. Chapter 10, the final chapter, offers a wealth of potential resources for the Early Years setting that practitioners may wish to access or purchase so that they can deliver the ideas put forward in this book.

Whilst this is meant to be a helpful guide for Foundation Stage trainees and practitioners it is merely a beginning. It is beyond the scope of this book to go into great detail about how to use ICT with young children. Likewise, issues concerning children with special educational needs in the Foundation Stage are not explored here. However, we have tried to balance the practicalities of teaching using ICT with the main pedagogical issues involved. We hope you find the book useful.

1 Using ICT in the Foundation Stage

In 1998 the DfEE (now DfES) set out new standards for trainee teachers in Circular 4/98 – *Teaching: High Status, High Standards*. It stated that:

> *ICT is more than just another teaching tool. Its potential for improving the quality and standards of pupils' education is significant.*

These standards have now been superseded by Circular 02/02 (*Qualifying to Teach* – DfES/TTA, 2002) but we believe that the sentiments of that statement are still very true today, although the accent is very much on the word 'potential'. ICT has not yet transformed education in the way in which it was hoped it would, but there are signs that this transformation is happening in some schools and that, year on year, the number of schools in which ICT is making an impact on teaching and learning is growing. This will be true of Early Years settings also, with some further along the road to an ICT revolution than others.

Barriers to ICT fulfilling its potential to transform teaching and learning

What are the barriers to ICT reaching its full potential? Lack of resources is often quoted as one stumbling block. The government's commitment to the promotion of ICT to improve children's education is not in doubt. Since 1997 when they came to power £1.8 billion has been spent on ICT-related initiatives under the National Grid for Learning (NGfL) banner. It has seen primary schools resourced to a level similar to secondary schools. A report by the BESA (British Educational Suppliers Association) (2002) confirmed that in 2001 the number of computers in British schools reached the one million mark. The growth in ICT resources has been tremendous and is set to continue. The age and quality of some of those resources may not always be what we would like, but there is much cause for optimism as far as this particular issue is concerned.

A lack of training is often cited by teachers as hindering the adoption of ICT in their lessons. The government has tackled this issue as part of its raft of measures to promote ICT in schools. Since 2001 trainee teachers have not been awarded Qualified Teacher Status (QTS) unless they have passed the ICT skills test and proven, through the duration of their course, that they can use ICT both in the teaching of subjects and for their own professional purposes. Those who qualified before that date have had the option to receive ICT training through the New Opportunities Fund (NOF) scheme whereby £230 million of lottery money was earmarked – supposedly the biggest government initiative since gas masks were issued to the public in World War Two! The success of this has been 'patchy'. The main aim of the NOF training was to promote the use of ICT in classroom practice and not, specifically, to develop teachers' ICT skills. Yet the training seems to have achieved the latter rather than the former. An OFSTED report (2002) says that the training has 'not had an impact in classrooms yet' but admits that teachers' ICT capability has increased and as a consequence that of their pupils has also improved. Again, we think that there is reason to be optimistic and are heartened by the fact that teachers' ICT skills are developing so well. That is good because we certainly subscribe to the view that teachers should be good role models for their charges when it comes to demonstrating confidence and competence in ICT in their everyday work.

Of course, a major barrier to ICT fulfilling its potential has always been the attitude of the teaching profession to ICT. The BESA report (2002) stated that over 60 per cent of teachers now feel 'confident and competent' when using computers. We all recognise the ICT-resistant (or downright anti-ICT!) members of staff but they are a dying breed. Rebecca Smithers, writing for the *Guardian*, reported that in a BT survey (2001) an overwhelming 98 per cent of teachers said that technology improved the quality of their teaching, whilst 95 per cent believed it boosted pupil attainment. This view was confirmed by the aforementioned OFSTED report (2002) into the effect of the government's ICT initiatives when it stated that:

> *There is now an unprecedented willingness in the teaching profession to embrace ICT and newly qualified teachers accept ICT as an integral part of their professional life.*

So whilst admitting there are substantial barriers to ICT fulfilling its potential to revolutionise teaching and learning there is much to be positive about. The good practice in those schools leading the way to educational transformation will become, we are confident, widespread during the next decade. The barriers are being lifted and this is no less true in the Foundation Stage setting.

The impact of ICT on learning

Computers have been in schools for over 20 years now. At first, evidence of their impact on educational standards tended to be impressionistic and anecdotal. However, things have changed. The government is spending millions of pounds on ICT in schools because of the positive research findings published in recent years. We do not intend to do an extensive review of that research in this book, but some of more recent and prominent research findings do warrant discussion.

A report by BECTa (2000), based on data from OFSTED inspections in 2,500 English primary schools, seemed strongly to suggest that there is a positive relationship between schools with 'good ICT resources' and high standards of achievement. A further report by BECTa (2001) confirmed these findings and explored other avenues of analysis. It concluded that besides 'the availability of good-quality ICT resources' there were four more 'critical factors' that good ICT learning is dependent upon. These are:

- good school leadership;
- a good general standard of teaching;
- good management of ICT as a subject;
- good classroom teaching of ICT.

Although this research did not focus upon the Early Years we believe that these factors apply equally to Foundation Stage practitioners and children.

Another piece of high-profile research into the effect of ICT on children's attainment is the ImpaCT2 study. The interim findings of this longitudinal study (1999–2002) are interesting despite the fact that it refers to Key Stage 2 children (and above). For example, it contends that a computer at home can be beneficial to children's education – this, we believe, is true for children in the 3–5-year-old bracket. It also states that:

> *ICT is not being used to its full potential to transform learning and teaching. Teachers need opportunities for reflective practice to embed innovation and change.* (BECTa 2001)

This reiterates what we have said in this chapter so far and applies to many Early Years practitioners as well as to teachers in general.

Specific research into the effect of ICT on the learning of Foundation Stage children has been thin on the ground. However, we can point to some useful studies. Findings from a research project by the University of Newcastle (1999), sponsored by the TTA, about the effect of ICT on learning in literacy and numeracy, did include younger children. They came to the conclusion that *ICT offers the potential to improve standards of attainment in literacy and mathematics.*

Interestingly, that word 'potential' pops up again! The study included an example of a Reception class teacher using ICT to develop counting skills. Using a painting program she was able to aid the development of the children's number recognition and writing skills, to consolidate their knowledge of the sequence of number names and ultimately to improve their counting skills.

Grenier and Thornbury (2001) did a small-scale study looking at the *joint attention* of adults and nursery children at the computer. This is a particularly worthy area of study as many researchers and theorists contend that it is always preferable to have an adult (be it the teacher, a parent or classroom assistant) at the computer with the child/ children to provide the all-important guidance and support (what

Bruner called 'scaffolding') essential to effective learning. This added value to past studies by Medwell (1996) and Collins *et al.* (1997) that suggested guided participation and purposeful intervention by adults when children are sitting at the computer in the Early Years setting is something that practitioners should always plan for.

A study by Pange and Kontozisis (2001) of Greek preschool children and the collaborative use of computers found that they offered quite a lot when it came to learning new concepts and gaining new knowledge. They based their work on Vygotsky's socio-cultural theory of learning where children's communication with their teachers and their peers is paramount. As well as these interactions being of prime importance, external tools, which could be interpreted today as the computer and other ICT devices, are also key factors in the children's learning. They applied Vygotsky's constructivist principles to their study. These included his well-known Zone of Proximal Development (ZPD) – the gap between what is already learnt and what the individual has the potential to learn. The gap can be bridged with the help of 'scaffolding' from teachers and more knowledgeable peers and implies children should not be alone when involved in ICT-based activities. He believed learning and development is a social activity. By collaborating in various ways with, around and through the computer the learner is more able to make educational gains. One of the major outcomes of this study by Pange and Kontozisis was the 'collaborative patterns that children developed while working with the computer'. More experienced children helped those with little or no experience. The latter children were not afraid to ask their 'mentors' questions. Other studies bear this out and practitioners will do well to take note. As Ager (1998, p18) puts it:

> *Collaborative work between two or three children in front of a computer working on any type of problem-solving activity can create an environment in which children within the group can provide scaffolding that they each need in order to progress.*

A recent study by John and Iram Siraj-Blatchford (2002), based on research carried out at 14 UK early learning centres (each with computers, educational software and specially designed furniture), found that children appreciated ICT when it was used for real-life purposes. We think this is significant as computers are seen by children, even very young children, as part of everyday life. Play seems more authentic if real, not 'pretend', apparatus is used and if that apparatus, for example the computer, is used to produce things that are really needed (like Mother's Day cards, for instance). The research concluded that children as young as 3 who use computers find it easier to understand technology and to develop their creative skills.

However, there are those who are not convinced of the worth of using computers with young children. Grenier and Thornbury (2001) cite the views of Kathy Sylva (a researcher in Early Years) who is of the opinion that computers restrict the development of creativity. A key finding in her research saw computers as a distraction. No doubt her views would be supported by the American organisation, Alliance for Childhood (2000), who felt that the benefits of computers for preschool children were 'vastly overstated'. Their report told of the physical harm computers could do and of the need for physical play rather than sitting glued to the PC screen.

Whilst we can see that care needs to taken in giving Foundation Stage children a wide range of experience, to deny them access to such a powerful, all-pervasive device would be wrong. Even the Alliance for Childhood recognises the usefulness of computers in giving children with special needs access to education. Furthermore, the motivational value of ICT is so obvious to practising teachers and so well documented now by researchers that it would be foolish indeed to ignore the *potential* power of using ICT in the Foundation Stage.

RESEARCH SUMMARY

Hall and Higgins (2002) focused on the findings of the major study (mentioned above) by the University of Newcastle looking at the effectiveness of computers in mathematics and English with regard to Early Years practitioners' beliefs and practices. Their analysis indicated that the attainment (or 'value added') of children of those Reception class teachers who were sceptical about the potential of ICT (and who lacked computer skills themselves) was 'significantly higher'. Hall and Higgins did not interpret this as meaning computers were disadvantageous to learning but that it was teachers' beliefs that were influencing the use of computers. Interestingly, though perhaps not surprisingly, these teachers tended to be the 'more experienced' practitioners. The more recently qualified Reception teachers had higher levels of computer skills and were more likely to use computers for three types of activity, namely, information retrieval, for children who had finished their work or as a free-choice activity. However, Hall and Higgins doubt that this practice is the best way forward. Their take on all this is that the use of computers is best when there are clear learning objectives for young children to work towards and the ICT activity is an integrated part of other teaching and learning strategies.

The ELG for ICT (pp 92–3 of the guidance) makes it clear that Early Years children should learn ICT to support their learning. They cross a number of 'stepping stones' to achieve this. These are:

- *showing an interest in ICT (including everyday technology such as radios, bar-code readers and pedestrian crossings);*
- *knowing how to operate simple equipment (like everyday devices such as television, video players and audio cassette players);*
- *completing a simple program on the computer (for example, giving instruction to a turtle);*

- *performing simple functions on ICT apparatus (such as taking a photograph using a digital camera).*

This is all very well but what, precisely, is the best way to develop ICT to support children's learning? We surfed over to BECTa's recently launched 'ICT Advice' website (**www.ictadvice.org.uk/**) and they offer some very helpful guidelines.

- *Ensure that a range of ICT resources is available in your setting.*
- *Encourage progression by introducing ICT resources as part of children's free play.*
- *Arrange the classroom so that all can see the computer monitor.*
- *Situate a computer in the role-play area if possible.*
- *Label ICT resources with stickers saying 'keyboard', 'printer', 'television' etc.*
- *Provide opportunities for children to work as a whole class, in groups, in pairs and as individuals with ICT-based resources.*
- *Introduce new ICT skills alongside other activities (for example, using a mouse whilst working with a maths CD-ROM).*
- *Develop ways of encouraging participation during whole-class sessions (especially with regard to using the correct vocabulary).*
- *When Early Years children are using the internet they should always be supervised.*

This all seems sound advice indeed and we concur that adopting such an approach in your Early Years setting could well bring dividends. Weeks (2000) came up with some sensible, practical strategies for teaching ICT in the Early Years at the end of her small-scale study that looked at the way in which it was taught in a Nursery class and a Reception class. She concluded that:

- *collaboration between the practitioners and assistants was vital;*
- *time should be spent familiarising oneself with software before using it with children;*
- *the correct vocabulary should be fostered from entry into the school;*
- *the correct way of using the equipment should be promoted from entry into the school;*

- *the left-hand mouse button should be marked with a coloured sticker;*
- *software should be chosen carefully, be intellectually stimulating and correlate with ongoing work in the classroom;*
- *the children should sit in pairs at the keyboard preferably with the teacher/assistant directly behind and between them;*
- *positive reinforcement should be used to encourage good behaviour and to reward achievements;*
- *children (and teachers!) will benefit from visual aids by the computer (and other ICT devices) to help with software and hardware operation;*
- *ensure equal use of the computer by having a name chart in class for children to record their usage.*

In our opinion, and in our experience, these are all excellent nuggets of advice. If we are to promote the laying of a firm foundation (in the appropriately named 'Foundation Stage') for young children's future learning and utilisation of ICT, then practitioners could do worse than adopt these strategies.

The six areas of learning and ICT

Although only overtly mentioned in one area of learning (Knowledge and Understanding of the World), it is clear from the Foundation Stage guidance that ICT should be used *to develop skills across [all] the areas of learning* (p 93). By ICT we are not talking just about computers but many devices such as printers, scanners, digital cameras, CD players, programmable robots, CD-ROMs and a variety of software packages – the list goes on! Practitioners should be aware of this when planning in each area of learning and they should bear in mind that ICT skills should be taught through the areas of learning rather than in isolation.

In the guidance (p 93), Foundation Stage teachers are advised to:

- *give opportunities for the use of ICT to develop skills across the areas of learning;*
- *encourage children to observe and talk about the use of ICT in the environment;*
- *encourage children to show each other how to use ICT equipment.*

What follows is a review of the kinds of resources that might be utilised under each area of learning. Later in this book we shall be attaching a theme to each of these areas of learning to illustrate how ICT can be used effectively.

Personal, Social and Emotional Development

The computer is a great help here as it encourages the children to collaborate and co-operate. The screen becomes the focus for group work and it maintains their attention and increases concentration as they develop their relationships with their peers. Vygotsky, a great proponent of the communicative approach to learning, would no doubt approve of this classroom resource being used in such a way. The computer, perhaps running a CD-ROM with the 'full multimedia monty' of colourful graphics, engrossing animations and amusing sound effects, will grab their interest, motivate learning and develop self-esteem. One of the advantages of using ICT devices is that children can almost always achieve success by getting it to do what they want it to. They can work as a team, perhaps using an adventure game, making decisions and solving problems. They can show their friends what they have achieved on the computer and help them to achieve similar results by demonstrating or helping them when they make mistakes. As well as computers and CD-ROMs, other ICT resources that might be used here include digital cameras, video cameras and tape recorders.

Communication, Language and Literacy

Not surprisingly there are endless opportunities to make use of ICT in this particular area, not least by Reception class teachers who must address the National Literacy Strategy (NLS) objectives. Stories and rhymes can be presented in the form of talking books on CD-ROMs, audio cassettes, on-screen 'big books' and interactive websites featuring favourite book and TV characters. There will be opportunities for role play where ICT plays an important part (for example, the school office, the library, the shop and so on). Speaking and listening skills can be encouraged by a group using adventure games on the computer or by them using a programmable robot to stimulate discussion as they solve a problem. Early literacy skills such as learning the alphabet and letter recognition can be developed using content-specific software. Early attempts at writing can be done using a simple word processor, preferably with the facility to 'talk'. A wordbank is also essential and an overlay keyboard, to input the text more quickly, may be useful too. E-mail could also be introduced here, perhaps with links being forged with another setting.

Mathematical Development

Here, too, where the demands of the National Numeracy Strategy (NNS) must also be met by Reception teachers, there is plenty of scope for making use of ICT resources. Content-specific software on a range of early numeracy topics is now available. Most are of the motivating multimedia type and similar things exist on the web. These CD-ROMs and websites help the development of counting skills and number recognition. Early learning in addition and subtraction will also be catered for. Calculators with larger keypads can also be used. Programmable robots are mentioned several times in the Foundation Stage guidance and although they can be used in other areas of learning it is in this particular one that they can be utilised the most. If you are exploring shape, space, measurement or even addition and subtraction, this toy can help children to develop mathematical skills. Older children in this age phase can try data handling by using one of the many simple graphing programs on the market. A sorting program would also prove useful.

Knowledge and Understanding of the World

Specific reference is made to ICT under this area of learning and practitioners are told to encourage children to show an interest in ICT, to see that they know how to operate simple equipment and instil the ability to complete a simple program and/or perform simple functions on ICT apparatus. These Early Learning Goals (ELGs) may well be achieved through work done in other areas of learning – as a glance at the text above will illustrate! This area of learning also *forms the foundation for later work in science, design and technology, history [and] geography* (p 82). There will be opportunities to use a variety of CD-ROMs and websites devoted to these subjects and topics within them. Role-play scenarios of everyday situations and outdoor play may well give opportunities to use a range of ICT devices.

Physical Development

There are CD-ROMs and websites aplenty that foster the development of mouse and keyboard skills. The guidance speaks of using 'one-handed tools' (p 114) and the mouse must be one of the most prolifically used one-handed tools in the world today! It is very important, not to say imperative, that young children learn to associate mouse movement with the pointer on the screen. Acquisition of this skill opens up a whole world of learning possibilities. A small mouse especially made for little hands is a useful resource worth your consideration. Awareness of health and the human body can be developed by making use of content-specific software and the web. Music cassettes, CDs and videos can be used to accompany movement. This might be an appropriate time to remind practitioners of the importance of flagging up health and safety issues with children regarding the use of and respect for ICT equipment. For example, children need to be made aware of the dangers of moving from the wet play area to an electrical appliance with wet hands!

Creative Development

This area of learning focuses on the development of art skills and musical ability. There is a wide choice of simple but powerful art programs out there today. They will delight the children as they doodle on the screen attempting to write their name or perhaps produce their first 'masterpiece'! Needless to say, a printer is essential if their efforts are to become hard copy, leading to increased self-esteem.

There are a number of music packages suitable for use by Foundation Stage children enabling them to play back familiar tunes and also to compose their own ditties. Electronic music keyboards can be introduced for more musical exploration. There are also many websites where favourite TV chums introduce children to the wonderful world of music. They would also find tape recorders, video and digital cameras very exciting as their own performances could be played back.

In conclusion

As we wrote this book in 2003 we visited the 'ICT in Schools' section of the DfES website (**www.dfes.gov.uk/ictinschools/index.shtml**) and found that the government's belief in the power of ICT is undiminished. It says, five years on from Circular 4/98, that:

> *ICT has the potential to completely transform teaching and learning over the next few years...*

Yet again, that word 'potential' is used. At the end of those five years will we still be talking about the *potential* of ICT to transform education? Or will we be talking about *reality*? We are not in the business of crystal-ball gazing but look forward to those five years with great hope.

This chapter has largely given the case *for* using ICT in the Foundation Stage setting. We make no bones about being supporters of its use. We acknowledge that there are barriers to ICT improving teaching and learning in the Early Years (as in all areas of education) but these can be and are being overcome. The evidence would suggest that the impact of ICT on standards of achievement in education in general seems to be significant and this would also appear to be the case in the Foundation Stage. We have outlined certain factors in good practice that practitioners would do well to adopt in their Early Years setting and reviewed ICT resources that can be used within each of the six areas of learning. Hopefully we have convinced the reader that using ICT in the Foundation Stage is worthwhile and will bring positive benefits if used in a meaningful way. In the words of Hall and Higgins (2002, p 293):

> *The burning questions are not **whether** computers should be used but **where** and **how** ICT can be used to enlarge and enrich young children's experience of learning.*

The *where* and *how* will be discussed in more detail in subsequent chapters.

2 Self-evaluation of needs

This chapter will make it possible for you to audit your current skills and practice with regard to ICT. It refers to the standards in *Qualifying to Teach* (DfES/TTA, 2002), and to Stepping Stones and Early Learning Goals in *Curriculum Guidance for the Foundation Stage* (QCD/DfEE, 2000). Trainee teachers of Foundation Stage children should find this a useful exercise and, we believe, established practitioners will also find this worthwhile. For each of the questions, posed below, answer 'Yes' or 'No'. Any questions where the response is the latter we would suggest needs addressing.

Self-audit of ICT skills for teaching the Foundation Stage

These skills refer to those needed if you are going to teach ICT effectively in the Early Years setting.

ACTIVITY

Answer 'Yes' or 'No' to the following questions.

Question	*Answer*
Are you competent and confident in using a computer?	
Are you familiar with a range of content-specific CD-ROMs suitable for use by Foundation Stage children across all six areas of learning?	
Are you familiar with a number of websites suitable for use by Foundation Stage children across all six areas of learning?	
Do you know how to use a programmable toy, such as Roamer, Pixie or Pip?	
Are you competent in using content-free software suitable for use with Foundation Stage children?	
Are you familiar with a word-processing package for young children with talking and wordbank facilities (e.g. *Clicker 4*)?	
Are you familiar with a graphing program (e.g. *Counting Pictures*)?	
Are you familiar with a painting program (e.g. *Kidpix Studio*)?	
Are you familiar with an object-based program (e.g. *My World*)?	
Are you familiar with a number of talking books and adventure games for Early Years children?	
Do you know how to use a range of ICT devices, including printers, scanners, digital cameras and audio equipment?	

Self-audit of ICT skills for professional purposes

All teachers should be able to make use of ICT for their own personal and professional use. This can improve your teaching and increase your efficiency. The use of *Microsoft Office* applications (or similar suites of programs) will be to the fore here.

ACTIVITY

Answer 'Yes' or 'No' to the following questions.

Question	*Answer*
Can you use a word processor or desktop publishing program to produce attractive teaching materials (e.g. worksheets, labels, posters, etc.)?	
Can you use a spreadsheet to keep records of attainment and progress?	
Can you use a presentation program to help you to deliver slick, entertaining lessons?	
Can you use e-mail to communicate with other practitioners or relevant outside agencies?	
Can you use the internet to join in professional discussions, to find and download teaching resources and to continue developing as a professional?	
Can you use administration and reporting software packages (e.g. PIPs) competently?	

Self-audit of practice with regard to the Early Learning Goal for ICT

A positive view by the Early Years practitioner towards ICT is essential if young children are to adopt a similar stance. Hall and Higgins (2002) observed that teachers' beliefs and attitudes about ICT had a direct effect on the way computers were used in the Early Years setting. A negative attitude would ultimately result in many children having an unenthusiastic view of technology. Try to answer these questions about your practice honestly.

ACTIVITY

Answer 'Yes' or 'No' to the following questions.

Question	*Answer*
Do you encourage children to show an interest in ICT?	
Do you give them opportunities to control programmable toys?	
Do you promote awareness of the technology around them?	
Do you stimulate every child's interest in ICT and other technology?	
Do you ensure the children know how to operate simple equipment?	
Do you teach the simple skills of using equipment?	

Do you help children understand how things work by giving them opportunities to disassemble and reassemble devices?	
Do you build on ICT skills that the children have developed at home?	
Do you encourage children to complete a simple program on the computer and allow them to perform simple functions on ICT apparatus?	
Do you teach and encourage the use of ICT in the setting?	
Do you provide opportunities in the role-play area to use ICT?	
Do you use language and terminology in conversations about ICT?	
Do you encourage children to discover and identify everyday technology and use ICT to support their learning?	
Do you give opportunities for the use of ICT to develop skills across all six areas of learning?	
Do you encourage children to observe and talk about the use of ICT in the environment?	
Do you encourage children to show each other how to use ICT equipment?	

Self-audit of practice with regard to other Early Learning Goals

Of course, if practitioners are indeed going to utilise ICT across the six areas of learning they should be alert to the opportunities and possibilities offered by other Early Learning Goals (ELGs). How good are you at looking for links between ELGs? For example, *Have a strong exploratory impulse* (Personal, Social and Emotional Development – p 32) equates nicely with *Show an interest in ICT* (Knowledge and Understanding of the World – p 92). There are plenty of links between the ELGs mentioned below and the requirements outlined in the ELG for ICT (pp 92–3). Some are more obvious than others.

ACTIVITY

Can you see an ICT-based activity that would aid the teaching (and learning) of these ELGs? As before, answer 'Yes' or 'No'.

Question	*Answer*
Personal, Social and Emotional Development	
Be confident to try new activities, initiate ideas and speak in a familiar group	
Work as part of a group, taking turns and sharing fairly	
Select and use activities and resources independently	
Communication, Language and Literacy	
Listen with enjoyment and respond to stories	
Hear and say initial and final sounds on words	
Write their own names and other things such as labels and captions	

Mathematical Development	
Recognise numerals 1 to 9	
Begin to relate addition to combining groups of objects	
Use everyday words to describe position	
Knowledge and Understanding of the World	
Find out about and identify some features of living things, objects and events they observe	
Ask questions about why things happen and how things work	
Find out about their environment	
Physical Development	
Recognise the importance of keeping healthy	
Recognise the changes that happen in their bodies when they are active	
Handle tools and objects	
Creative Development	
Explore colour, texture, shape, form and space	
Recognise how sounds can be changed	
Respond in a variety of ways to what they hear	

Self-audit of practice with regard to an OFSTED inspection

We thought practitioners would be interested in what OFSTED inspectors would expect to see, in terms of ICT, in the Foundation Stage setting. We visited BECTa's 'ICT Inspection' website (**www.becta.org.uk/supportproviders/inspection/index.html**) to ascertain what guidelines inspectors are given. The activity below provides a summary of this guidance for practitioners.

TIVITY

Answer 'Yes' or 'No' as above.

Question	*Answer*
Inspectors will be looking for evidence that practitioners and pupils use ICT in their daily lives	
Do you use ICT to record planning?	
Do you use ICT in displays around the classroom?	
Does planning include the use of ICT by both yourself and the children?	
Do you introduce the correct language when referring to ICT?	
Do you have evidence of children's use of ICT in their work and in role-play activities?	

Inspectors will be looking at the availability of ICT resources in the learning environment	
Do you have adequate and varied hardware (e.g. computers, printers, televisions, video players, cassette players, programmable toys, etc.) available in your setting?	
Do you have adequate and appropriate software (e.g. paint program, talking word-processor with wordbank facility, simple graphing package, talking story CD-ROMs, music CDs, etc.) available for use with that hardware?	
Inspectors will be looking at pupils' level of involvement with ICT	
Are the children passive receivers of the ICT around them?	
Do your pupils share the use of ICT when carrying out activities with each other or with you?	
Do your pupils use ICT independently?	
Inspectors will be looking at pupils' curriculum use of ICT	
Do the children control equipment (e.g. televisions, video players, cassette recorders, CD players, etc.) themselves?	
Are the children aware of control applications (e.g. remote control cars, programmable toys, the mouse, the computer keyboard, etc.) in school?	
Are the children aware of control applications (e.g. street lighting, traffic lights, telephones, barcode readers, etc.) in the home and wider environment?	
Do the children use ICT to present their work in the form of pictures and words?	
Do the children use ICT to find things out to support their learning?	

Evaluating the audit

Having completed your self-assessment audit the next step is to draw up an action plan. Look at the 'no's on your audit. Prioritise the list you compile. Take the first four or five issues. Address these and, having achieved your goals, move on to the next group on your list of priorities. This template may be of use.

Target area	Start date	Review date	Resources	Reading
1.				
2.				
3.				
4.				
5.				

You may well need certain resources – hardware, software and so on. Make sure these are available. Further reading may also be required – the rest of this book may prove helpful, as will be several sources in the recommended further reading section in Chapter 10.

In conclusion

Hopefully, by this point, you will have completed your self-audit. It looked at these areas:

- ICT skills for teaching the Foundation Stage;
- ICT skills for professional purposes;
- practice with regard to the Early Learning Goal for ICT;
- practice with regard to other Early Learning Goals;
- practice with regard to an OFSTED inspection.

Now the evaluating and action-planning part of the process begins. Good luck – we hope it proves worthwhile as part of your continuing professional development as a Foundation Stage practitioner. Next we move on to the thorny issue of managing ICT in the Early Years setting.

3 Managing ICT in the Foundation Stage

The purpose of this chapter is to help you explore the most effective ways of managing ICT in the Foundation Stage. This will include guidance about the practical issues you will be faced with, in particular with regard to planning, assessment, management and organisation.

The key to effective teaching and learning in the Early Years lies in practitioners' understanding and belief in the principles for Early Years education. These are clearly acknowledged in the *Curriculum Guidance for the Foundation Stage* (QCA.DfEE, 2000, pp 11–12).

- ***Effective education requires both a relevant curriculum and practitioners who understand and are able to implement the curriculum requirements.***
- ***Effective education requires practitioners who understand that children develop rapidly during the Early Years – physically, intellectually, emotionally and socially.*** *Children are entitled to provision that supports and extends knowledge, skills, understanding and confidence, and helps them to overcome any disadvantage.*
- ***Practitioners should ensure that all children feel included, secure and valued.*** *They must build positive relationships with parents in order to work effectively with them and their children.*
- ***Early Years experience should build on what children already know and can do.*** *It should also encourage a positive attitude and disposition to learn and aim to prevent failure.*
- ***No child should be excluded or disadvantaged*** *because of ethnicity, culture or religion, home language, family background, special educational needs, disability, gender or ability.*
- ***Parents and practitioners should work together*** *in an atmosphere of mutual respect within which children can have security and confidence.*
- ***To be effective, an Early Years curriculum should be carefully structured****. In that structure, there should be three strands:*
  - *provision for the different starting points from which children develop their learning, building on what they can already do;*
  - *relevant and appropriate content that matches the different levels of young children's needs;*

  – *planned and purposeful activity that provides opportunities for teaching and learning, both indoors and outdoors.*

- ***There should be opportunities for children to engage in activities planned by adults and also those that they plan or initiate by themselves.*** *Children do not make a distinction between 'play' and 'work' and neither should practitioners. Children need time to become engrossed, work in depth and complete activities.*
- ***Practitioners must be able to observe and respond appropriately to children,*** *informed by a knowledge of how children develop and learn and a clear understanding of possible next steps in their development and learning.*
- ***Well planned, purposeful activity and appropriate intervention by practitioners will engage children in the learning process*** *and help them make progress in their learning.*
- ***For children to have rich and stimulating experiences, the learning environment should be well planned and well organised.*** *It provides the structure for teaching within which children explore, experiment, plan and make decisions for themselves, thus enabling them to learn, develop and make good progress.*
- ***Above all, effective learning and development for young children requires high-quality care and education by practitioners.***

Regardless of the area of learning a child is experiencing, the support and guidance we give to children should reflect these principles at all times. Throughout this chapter, we will look explicitly at how these principles are adopted in the context of ICT.

The remainder of this chapter will look at how ICT can be managed in the Foundation Stage, with a consideration of the principles of good Early Years practice.

Providing a meaningful context for children to learn

- *Effective education requires both a relevant curriculum and practitioners who understand and are able to implement the curriculum requirements.*
- *Effective education requires practitioners who understand that children develop rapidly during the Early Years – physically, intellectually, emotionally and socially.*

Children learn in different ways and at different rates. We know that this is due to a number of reasons. Some children have been exposed to a wide range of experiences which have provided them with opportunities to develop holistically. Other children may have had more limited experiences, or have specific learning difficulties. All these factors will have an impact on the level of knowledge, skills and attitudes children bring with them to your Early Years setting.

This has implications for practitioners when considering how we implement ICT in our settings. The expectations we have of children should reflect our understanding of how children will use ICT. For example, it would be inappropriate to expect a child with limited language development to retell a story on to a tape recorder. This child would benefit more from being exposed to stories and rhymes through, perhaps, listening to them on an audio tape or CD-ROM. On the other hand, there may be another child in your setting who is confident and articulate in both speaking and listening, who would be much more suited to the retelling story activity.

It is also important that we are aware of the requirements of children with special educational needs and learning difficulties. The benefits of ICT in this area are often quoted and we would agree that it can be invaluable in giving children with special educational needs access to the curriculum. We would urge practitioners to visit the NGfL's 'Inclusion' website (**inclusion.ngfl.gov.uk/**) to gain access to many ICT resources for use with these children. A quick search on the BECTa site and the ICT Advice site will yield much information on using ICT with children who have physical disabilities, learning and behavioural difficulties, as well gifted and talented children.

We will discuss the notion of flexibility and our role in supporting children later in the chapter but, at this point, let's consider how we can provide a meaningful context for children's learning. There are a number of principles that make reference to our partnership with parents:

- ***Practitioners should ensure that all children feel included, secure and valued.***
- ***No child should be excluded or disadvantaged*** *because of ethnicity, culture or religion, home language, family background, special educational needs, disability, gender or ability.*
- ***Parents and practitioners should work together*** *in an atmosphere of mutual respect within which children can have security and confidence.*

There is sometimes a danger that, as practitioners, we presume that we are 'the experts' and we know everything there is to know about young children and how they learn. Yet a child's parents hold the key to a wealth of information about their child that we may never know – unless we endeavour to find out! This can lead to us to making judgements about a child which are in fact incorrect. For example, is a child from a wealthy background necessarily going to have been exposed to the use of a computer more than a child who lives with a lone parent receiving benefit?

Consider all the children in your current setting – do you know the answers to the following questions? Which children:

- have a computer at home?
- can operate the remote control for their video/DVD player?
- have access to the internet at home?
- have remote control toys at home?
- regularly answer the telephone?
- can write their name using upper case letters on the computer?
- regularly accompany their parents to the supermarket and can tell you how a 'scanner' works?
- have parents who have good ICT skills, and which children have parents with limited ICT skills?
- listen to story tapes at bedtime?

In order to ensure that we provide a meaningful context for learning and that all children have equality of opportunity which will allow them to develop further at their own rate, these are the type of questions we need to know the answers to.

Once we have this information, we can consider ways of working with parents that will further support children's learning. For example, workshops with parents can serve a number of purposes. They can be used to support parents' own learning and development, or as a way of sharing with parents how they can support their child's learning at home.

ACTIVITY

Consider the children and families in your setting. What could you do, first, to find out about children's ICT experiences at home? Secondly, how will you use this information to ensure that the ICT experiences you provide in your setting are both relevant and meaningful and that all children feel included, secure and valued?

Play and ICT

- ***There should be opportunities for children to engage in activities planned by adults and also those that they plan or initiate by themselves.*** *Children do not make a distinction between 'play' and 'work' and neither should practitioners. Children need time to become engrossed, work in depth and complete activities.*

When children are playing, they have ownership of what they are doing and so are intrinsically motivated to learn. As a result of this, children will develop and reinforce new knowledge, skills and understanding.

Additionally they may be more likely to problem solve and take risks.

Consider the following two scenarios, both of which involve Sam, who is four years old:

> Sam is sitting with an adult who is 'teaching' him how to write his name on the computer. She directs him to the relevant keys that correspond to his name. When he has successfully completed that, she shows him how to click on the 'print' button. When his name is printed out, he is instructed to stick his piece of paper in his writing book – then he can go and 'choose' something to play with. Meanwhile, the adult asks another child who is currently playing in the sand to come and do his 'computer work'.
>
> Sam is playing in the post office. The computer is located in the post office, and set up with a simple word-processing package. Sam is busy 'writing' a letter to Father Christmas on the computer. When he gets to the end of the letter, he says to the adult who is also playing in the area, 'Look, I writed my name. How do I make it come out on a piece of paper?' The adult guides Sam to the 'print' icon, and Sam prints out his letter, folds it into an envelope and then posts it. A short while later, another child – Rachel – also uses the computer to write a letter. She is unsure of how to print out her letter. Sam takes great delight in showing Rachel how to click and print.

What knowledge, skills, understanding and attitudes do you think Sam learnt in the two scenarios? Earlier in this chapter we talked about the importance of providing a meaningful context for learning. For young children, play experiences provide an opportunity for children to practise and develop new skills in a meaningful context. How likely do you think it would be that Sam would wish to replicate his experiences in the first scenario – and, more importantly, make a connection with what the adult intended him to learn in a different context? In the second scenario, Sam had ownership of what he was doing and, because of that he made a genuine connection with the concept of writing through the medium of the computer.

We are not suggesting that you just let children 'play', and hope they learn some ICT skills along the way. Our responsibility is to ensure that we provide a balance of opportunities for both adult- and child-initiated learning within the daily routine. This should help us ensure that children will have planned opportunities to develop specific skills, but also time to practise the skills in a way which will be of benefit to the child. Chapters 4–9 provide further support related to how this can look in practice.

The role of the adult

Another important feature of the two scenarios was the role of the adult in relation to supporting children's learning:

- ***Well planned, purposeful activity and appropriate intervention by practitioners will engage children in the learning process*** *and help them make progress in their learning.*

In the first scenario, the adult was instructing Sam in a rather didactic way. There was little evidence of any sensitive interaction – or 'scaffolding'. It could be argued that the process was rather mechanical, and the adult was only concerned with achieving an end product, which could be saved as 'evidence' of the child's learning.

In the second scenario, the adult was much more sensitive. She was aware of the Zone of Proximal Development which Sam had reached, and was therefore able to provide the support he needed in order to help him move forward. She did not intervene with Sam's learning, until she was invited. Even then, she only provided the support that Sam requested. This enabled him to make progress and succeed. As a result of this, Sam demonstrated his new knowledge by then showing Rachel how to print out her own writing. Although the adult's help was not requested at this point, it was evident that her earlier intervention was all that was needed to help him make progress in his learning.

Planning the curriculum

Another important role of the adult is to provide well-planned activities. There are two further principles which relate to this:

- ***Early Years experience should build on what children already know and can do.*** *It should also encourage a positive attitude and disposition to learn and aim to prevent failure.*
- ***To be effective, an Early Years curriculum should be carefully structured****. In that structure, there should be three strands:*
  - *provision for the different starting points from which children develop their learning, building on what they can already do;*
  - *relevant and appropriate content that matches the different levels of young children's needs;*
  - *planned and purposeful activity that provides opportunities for teaching and learning, both indoors and outdoors.*

We have already discussed in some detail the importance of planning experiences within a meaningful context. It is vital that, as practitioners, we have sufficient knowledge about what children already know and have experienced.

The greatest challenge for Early Years practitioners is planning experiences that take account of the different developmental needs of all children. It is therefore vital that planned experiences are both flexible and open ended enough to meet the needs of all children. In the examples that we provide in the following chapters, the learning objectives are based on the ELGs. You may well find that these are not always appropriate due to the age or stage of development of the children you are working with. Activities can be differentiated in a number of ways. By:

- level of adult support (e.g. working with smaller groups or individual children when using a digital camera);
- task (e.g. reducing the complexity of the activity such as using pictures on a concept keyboard instead of text);
- outcome (e.g. placing greater emphasis on exploration rather than an end product such as a printout);
- resources (e.g. using a toy such a remote-control car rather than a programmable robot).

There can sometimes be a temptation to plan an activity which leads to an end product, with the idea that this then provides the 'evidence' for learning. As a result, learning can sometimes become no more than a production line (such as in Scenario 1), where the aim is to ensure all children have experienced the 'task'. The process of learning is far more important than the end product. During this time children are usually socially engaged with either their peers or a supportive adult. It is the process of active learning and social interaction that enables children to learn. ICT is actually a wonderful vehicle for children to become socially engaged, as it is necessary for children to talk to each other, negotiate, take turns and problem solve.

Therefore, when planning experiences, think about the most meaningful context for children to learn specific skills, which are flexible enough to take account of the different rate at which children learn. The Stepping Stones in the curriculum guidance provide an excellent tool for helping you determine the different developmental levels children are at, and therefore plan appropriate experiences. These are important as the early experiences children encounter as they begin the Foundation Stage provide the essential building blocks for future learning. Remember also, it is far better to focus on supporting children in developing one or two specific skills each term, and making sure they have many opportunities to use and apply those skills within that time. One of the most rewarding aspects of effective planning is when children are seen to take their learning forward during their child-initiated play, where the original starting point of your first planned experience has been incorporated into their own play. This is authentic proof that you have provided a starting point that is meaningful, relevant and interesting to your children.

The next six chapters in this book provide examples of popular themes under each area of learning. They are intended to illustrate how ICT can be addressed across the curriculum although, as you will see, it is impossible to isolate one area of learning completely and links to other areas are highlighted. The examples we have given could provide a useful starting point for planning further experiences to expand the topic and cover the other areas of learning in greater depth. For detailed guidance about planning in the Foundation Stage visit the QCA website (**www.qca.org.uk/ca/foundation/planning_for_learning.asp**), which provides advice on short, medium and long-term planning.

The themes we have chosen could constitute a whole year's ICT experiences and form part of a long-term plan:

- 'Under the Ground' (KUW)
- *The Jolly Postman* (CLL)
- 'Going Shopping' (MD)
- 'All About Me' (PSED)
- 'Let's Move!' (PD)
- 'Stars and Moons' (CD).

We developed our own medium and short-term planning templates based on others we have seen.

MEDIUM-TERM PLAN

Area of learning	Learning objectives	Possible experiences	Resources

SHORT-TERM PLAN

Focus	
Main area of learning	
Learning objectives	
Prior learning	
Activity	
Resources	
Adult role	
ICT skills to be developed	
Assessment opportunities	
Follow-up activities	
Links with other areas of learning	

These are the models we have used in the next six chapters. You may like to use them or adapt them to suit your own needs.

Assessment

- ***Practitioners must be able to observe and respond appropriately to children,*** *informed by a knowledge of how children develop and learn and a clear understanding of possible next steps in their development and learning.*

Another important role that we have as practitioners is related to assessment. This is the key to good-quality planning. We have discussed the importance of providing experiences that build upon what children already know and can do. Sharing information with parents is one way of determining a starting point for your planning, but we also need to know what children have learnt during their time spent engaged in adult- and child-initiated learning experiences. Once we have this information, we can plan further experiences which build on what children already know.

The most important assessment tool that Early Years practitioners should use is observation. *Watching* how children interact and use ICT and *listening* to what they say helps us to understand more about a child's interest and capability. Once we are clear of this, we can intervene with sensitive questioning and other interaction strategies – if appropriate – which may give us a further insight into a child's capabilities. It is important that we observe children during their play, as well as in our planned activities. As mentioned earlier in this chapter, children's play gives us a more genuine insight into a child's ability to apply ICT skills in a meaningful context.

Making judgements about children's ICT capability during child-initiated play is sometimes rather difficult. An Early Years setting is always a very busy place with a lot of interesting things happening at any one time. Therefore, there are going to be occasions when you miss a crucial ICT moment where a child may have demonstrated a very specific skill. If you have a consistent daily routine, where there are regular opportunities for children to review and talk about what they have done during their child-initiated activities, this will be the ideal opportunity to make an assessment. By asking children to talk about what they have done – for example, 'How did you make the computer print your picture?' – they should either be able to articulate or demonstrate on the machine what they actually did. Not only will they be providing evidence for your assessment – but also teaching their peers!

The Foundation Stage profile, which has replaced Baseline Assessment, specifically requires practitioners carefully to observe children in a variety of contexts. This information can then be used to make informed judgements about a child's stage of development in each area of learning.

In order to make your assessment manageable, it is important to identify in your short-term planning a clear objective related to ICT capability, which will form the focus of your assessment. The examples in Chapters 4–9 should illustrate this for you. Using the Stepping Stones as guidance, you should then be able to make a judgement about a child's developmental level and, in turn, identify what further experiences children need next to take them forward in their learning.

Management and organisation

- ***For children to have rich and stimulating experiences, the learning environment should be well planned and well organised.*** *It provides the structure for teaching within which children explore, experiment, plan and make decisions for themselves, thus enabling them to learn, develop and make good progress.*

The way in which we manage and organise the learning environment can have a huge impact on the extent to which children use ICT in their everyday learning. The first consideration is the range of resources that we make available for children to use. Let's consider what we should be providing for children to use.

Everyday technology

We now live in a society immersed in technological gadgets and devices. Children are exposed to these in their everyday life. Therefore, we should ensure that the resources we have in our settings reflect children's own lives – in that way they will be able to make authentic connections between real life and imagination during their play. It is important that we provide as many 'real' objects for children to use as possible, rather than the manufactured and some times poorly replicated plastic alternatives. Children need to be able to use these types of objects in two ways. First, as objects to be used in role-play and, secondly, to be able to take apart and put together.

The following list is by no means finite but should provide you with a starting point. Remember that any electrical goods need to have plugs and other dangerous parts removed:

- landline and mobile telephone;
- remote-control handset;
- audio tape recorder;
- kitchen equipment (e.g. toasters, microwave);
- microphone;
- computer keyboard;
- redundant camera;
- TV set;
- cash register/scanner.

An important aspect of children's learning in relation to ICT is the concept that performing a function – such as pressing a button – elicits a certain response. Therefore, it is important that we also provide working resources that give children opportunities to do this. Resources such as remote control cars, digital camera, video and tape recorders should all be available for children to use in your setting. There is a comprehensive list of resources in Chapter 10 of this book that will provide you with more information.

One of the reasons why ICT was not always a feature in the Early Years setting was because of the limited range and use of programs available. That is no longer the case today! It is imperative that the practitioner is willing to invest time and effort in becoming familiar with the range of computer programs available. Additionally, time needs to be given over to actually setting up programs for children to be able to use successfully. This could be setting up a word-processing program for children to use in the role-play corner, finding relevant websites for children to access or downloading pictures that can easily be stored and retrieved. Once you have established a bank of resources, it becomes much easier to adapt them to fit in with your different projects. Before you know it, ICT will become an inherent part of your everyday life!

Once you are confident that your setting is resourced adequately, you now need to think about how the resources are actually going to be organised. Think about where and how you will locate your resources. It makes sense to locate them near other relevant areas of learning. Children are then more likely to use them in their play. For example, it makes sense to locate the computer near your writing area, with a 'Write' program set up and ready to use. Remember, though, the computer does not always have to be in the same area. By simply changing the location of the computer, the dynamics of children's play can change dramatically. You may decide that it could be used in the role-play area with a program that supports their imaginative play (see Chapter 7, for example).

One common problem with computers is that practitioners are sometimes concerned that some children only ever choose to use the computer when playing. This means that these children are potentially having a limited range of experiences in the setting, and that other children have very few opportunities to develop their ICT skills. The most important thing to consider in this type of situation is to ask, first, why this is happening? It could be for a number of reasons – a child's lack of confidence in engaging in other types of play, or wider social interaction or limited experiences of using computers outside the classroom. There are a number of possible solutions to this common problem.

- Move the computer to a different part of the classroom. By physically playing in a different part of the classroom it alerts children to other areas which they may not be aware actually exist, and may also introduce them to different types of play. (Role-play is a good example.)
- Use the 'frequent user' children to teach others. This is particularly useful when there are few adults in the classroom. The cascading effect is particularly useful if a program only requires a limited number of skills, which can easily be modelled by other more confident users.
- Turn the situation into a problem-solving situation. Hand the problem over to the children and ask what they think would be a reasonable solution.

Specialist ICT equipment for the Early Years setting can be purchased. Lower-case keyboards, graph pads and small mice spring to mind here. Alternative input devices could prove useful especially when used with SEN children. The apparatus you might consider using include switches, touchpads, trackerballs and joysticks. Software that produces a large pointer on-screen may also be a good idea, not just for a visually impaired child but for general use. For quick and easy text entry a concept keyboard is pretty much essential and the use of predictive word processors is advised. The 'accessibility' options in Windows is an alternative the practitioner can use to make the computer keyboard and mouse more friendly. Experiment with these and decide which settings are appropriate.

One final word related to management and organisation. Your role is vital in supporting children in their learning. Computers can be temperamental, and children do not have the innate fear of crashing programs as adults do. Therefore, although it is an ideal forum for them to explore and take risks, you have to be prepared to rectify any problems that may occur. This is why it is important to ensure that you are very familiar with the workings of a program, and all children are secure in using specific skills. Your time should be invested in providing children with a smaller range of quality experiences rather than a larger quantity of experiences where there is no assurance that children have actually learnt anything.

In conclusion

Please remember also that, when using the internet, you must ensure that an adult is always present. Indeed, whenever children are using a computer the presence of an adult is often preferable so that they can provide the all-important scaffolding needed to progress.

Now you have reached the end of this chapter, you should now feel more confident in actually managing ICT in your classroom. The key points to remember in all aspects of your practice are:

- children need to have meaningful experiences, which are relevant to their developmental needs and help them make connections with the real world and their own learning;
- the role of the adult is vital in planning and organising meaningful learning experiences, but also in supporting children's learning through sensitive and appropriate intervention;
- ICT is an excellent tool for providing children with active and social learning experiences – but it will only be successful if practitioners are willing to invest their time in making it work.

4 Knowledge and Understanding of the World: 'Under the Ground'

Our first theme is called 'Under the Ground' – a science-based topic that can be addressed within the Knowledge and Understanding of the World area of learning. Science is a subject that invariably affords much scope for the inclusion of ICT. After all, at this moment scientists all around the world are using computers to write reports, to run simulations, to research using the internet, to log and record data and to interrogate the results. We believe that children should emulate real scientists and use computers in their science work too. This work can begin in the Early Years setting.

There are many possibilities for using a wide variety of ICT devices here, and different software packages and websites too. Creatures that live under the ground can be identified and studied using suitable CD-ROMs such as *Amazing Animals* (Dorling Kindersley) and websites such as *Naturegrid* (**www.naturegrid.org.uk/**) (Figure 1). There will be television programs and videos available on this topic, and the opportunity to create their own videos using a camcorder.

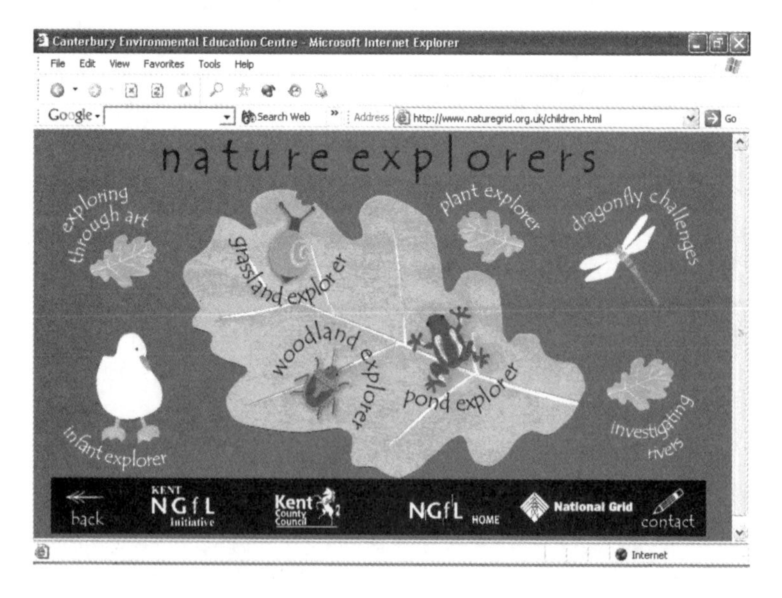

Figure 1 Explore *Naturegrid* to find out about animals

There will be opportunities for identifying, sorting and classifying animals and plants using a branching database to create a binary tree with a program such as *2question* (part of the *Infant Video Toolbox* by 2simple) or *FlexiTREE* (Flexible Software). This type of software enables the user to identify 'objects' (in this case animals and/or plants) by posing questions, the answer to which must be either 'yes' or 'no'. It also enables the user to learn the attributes of the object in question. This type of program can engender much valuable discussion as the children decide what the attributes are. For example, is a worm really slimy? Or does it just look that way? It really does help to develop and refine their questioning techniques (Figure 2).

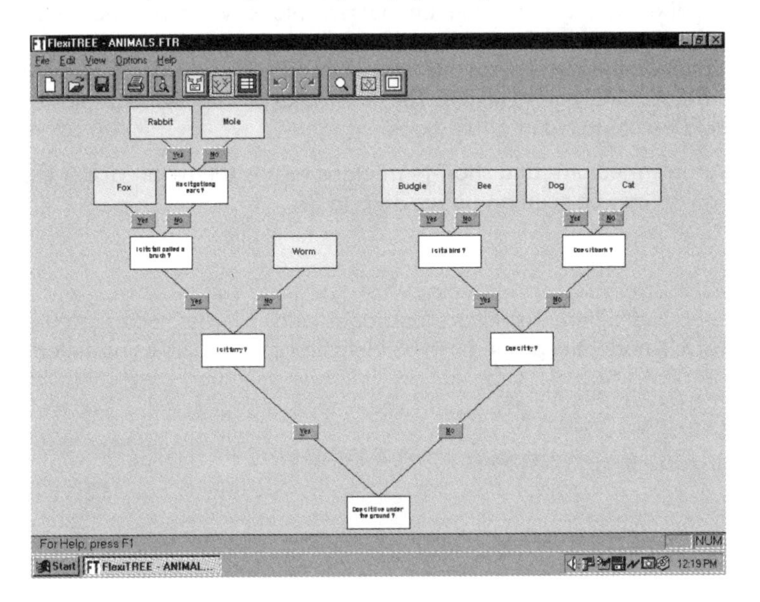

Figure 2 *FlexiTREE* – simple but effective sorting software

Our focus for this theme involves the use of a digital camera. The advantage of a digital camera, as opposed to a conventional camera, is that there is no waiting for the film to be developed and no need, once you have the photographs, to scan them into the computer. Digital cameras capture images electronically and store them as digital files until they are downloaded on to a computer for viewing, manipulating and printing. They are very common nowadays in schools and are particularly useful when recording educational visits and outdoor activities such as the one outlined below.

Photographs taken can be viewed on the liquid crystal display (LCD) and deleted if found to be substandard. Once you have all the pictures required the camera can be connected to the computer and often viewed with software that came with the camera itself. However, many graphics programs these days will do the job, although a powerful graphics manipulation program such as *Paintshop Pro* (JASC) would be even better. This program is far too sophisticated for children to use but a computer literate practitioner could use it *with* children to browse pictures. A free graphics viewer called *Irfan View* (www.irfanview.com) is also available and able to support common photographic formats such as JPEG.

The software should allow the children to view small versions of the photograph called 'thumbnails'. An image can be chosen, enlarged, cropped and other adjustments can be made before printing. Some of these packages will allow captions to be written on to the picture itself but if not they can always be produced with a word processor. In fact, the photographs can be pasted into a word-processing or desktop publishing package and both the image and its caption can appear on the same piece of paper. A decent colour inkjet printer will give surprisingly good results. They will make an impressive display or could be compiled in a 'big book'.

Example medium- and short-term plans for the theme of 'Under the ground' can be seen on pages 35 and 36.

MEDIUM-TERM PLAN

Area of learning	Learning objectives	Possible experiences	Resources
Knowledge and Understanding of the World	KUW 1: Use senses to explore the ground outside	• While exploring the ground outside use the digital camera to record experiences • Review pictures taken, print off and share sensory experiences • Write and print captions/labels for the photographs	Buckets, spades, rakes, sieves and sample containers Magnifying glasses Digital camera Printer Computer Graphics software Word-processing software
	KUW 1: Find out about and identify features of living things underground	• Use a CD-ROM such as *Amazing Animals* to identify creatures that live underground • View videos to find out about creatures • Visit websites to find out about plants and creatures	Printer Computer CD-ROMs Internet access TV/video
	KUW 1: Look at similarities, differences, patterns and change	• Use a branching database to sort and classify plants, creatures, etc, according to different properties • Use a sorting program on the internet at the MAPE website	Printer Computer Branching database software (e.g. *2 Question* – part of the Infant Video Toolkit) Internet access
	KUW 1: Ask questions about why things happen	• Use a CD-ROM to find out why certain creatures live underground • Also, use the internet to find answers to these questions • Plant seeds and track growth with a digital camera • Label plants using a simple word processor	Printer Computer CD-ROMS Internet access Digital camera Word-processing software
	KUW 5: Find out about their environment and talk about the features they like and dislike	• Use a video camera to record their views (likes/dislikes) of features of their nursery/school garden • Use a Clicker grid to make a plan of changes they would like to see in the garden	Video camera Printer Computer *Clicker 4* software

SHORT-TERM PLAN

Focus	'Under the Ground'
Main area of learning	Knowledge and Understanding of the World
Learning objectives	KUW 1: Use senses to explore the ground outside KUW 3: To perform simple functions on the computer using a mouse
Prior learning	• While exploring the ground outside using spades, rakes, magnifying glasses, etc., the children take photographs using the digital camera to record their experiences
Activity	• In small groups, with an adult, children view 'thumbnails' of the pictures taken during the previous session • Children then choose the photographs they wish to view full size • They can then print off a photograph each • Talk about individual pictures encouraging children to recall their sensory experiences
Resources	• Computer, digital camera (with USB cable), graphics software (e.g. *Paintshop Pro*), inkjet colour printer
Adult role	• Model and support appropriate ICT skills • Encourage the children to talk about their experiences in the garden using sensory language (i.e what they saw, what they felt, what they heard, what they smelt and possibly tasted!)
ICT skills to be developed	• Know how to operate a digital camera • Use a mouse to operate the graphics software
Assessment opportunities	• Can the child take a usable photograph? • Can the child move the mouse to select the picture, enlarge and print?
Follow-up activities	• Use a simple word-processing package to write and print captions/labels for the photographs • Make a display/book of the activity
Links with other areas of learning	• PSED 1: Be confident to try new activities, initiate ideas and speak in a familiar group • CLL 1: Interact with others, negotiating plans and activities and taking turns in conversation, speak clearly and audibly with confidence and control. . . • CLL 5: Attempt writing for different purposes • PD 5: Handle tools and objects safely and with increasing control

5 Communication, Language and Literacy: The Jolly Postman

This theme for Communication, Language and Literacy is based on the wonderful book by Janet and Allan Ahlberg, *The Jolly Postman*. If it's the appropriate time of year *The Jolly Christmas Postman* could also be used as a stimulus. Many characters from nursery rhymes and fairy tales are mentioned in these books (many of which will be familiar to some children) and this is used as a springboard for much exciting work and play.

There are various and numerous audio cassettes and CDs on the market today where traditional nursery rhymes are sung and popular fairy tales are read aloud. These will develop children's listening skills and spark conversation about the characters. There are plenty of CD-ROMs available too that will delight and motivate the children. 'All singing, all dancing' talking stories are very popular. Using the full range of multimedia features on offer today, these programs can charm even the most reluctant child:

> *Children today live in a 'multimedia' world: children's television programmes are confirmation of this. Very young children require computer programs to be bright, cheerful and easy to access if they are to remain interested. CD-ROMs, which store vast quantities of information incorporating text, pictures, sound and moving images, can be particularly powerful and motivating.*
>
> (BECTa 2001)

Two examples you might choose to use for this particular theme are *Nursery Rhyme Time* (Sherston) and *Rainbow Stories* (Resource). Websites offering multimedia versions of nursery rhymes and fairy tales, and often hosted by children's favourite TV characters, include *Teletubbies* (Figure 3) (**www.bbc.co.uk/cbeebies/teletubbies/nurseryrhymes/**), *Tweenies* (**www.bbc.co.uk/cbeebies/tweenies/storytime/**) and *Cbeebies Stories* (**www.bbc.co.uk/cbeebies/stories/**). These represent a handful of the resources out there. A browse through a software catalogue or around the web can bring dividends.

The use of programmable robots will be discussed in more depth in the next chapter (on Mathematical Development) but they do bear mentioning at this point as they are an excellent tool for promoting speaking and listening skills. You will notice below that we have suggested using the Roamer as the Jolly Postman (you can even dress it up if you wish!), delivering his letters as a means of getting the children talking, listening to each other's ideas and coming to some sort of consensus about the instructions to give. Clare and David Mills (1997) suggested that too much time was being spent on the '3 Rs'

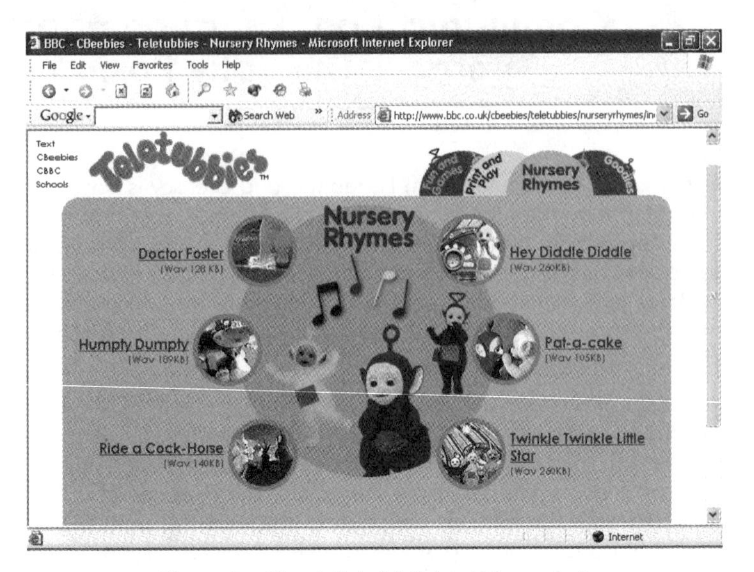

Figure 3 The delightful *Teletubbies* website

even at the Foundation Stage. Their research showed that very little spoken language was going on between children and, indeed, between children and adults, in the Early Years setting. Carol Fine and Mary Lou Thornbury (1998) tried to address this problem by using 'control', in the form of a programmable robot called 'Pip', to foster task-related talk in the nursery. In their words:

> *Our experience in using control [the floor robot Pip] in the Early Years is that children talk and listen, revise and review, and evaluate and refine the use of their language in order to be understood and to achieve their joint goals.*

So it would seem that a programmable toy, or floor robot, can be invaluable in promoting spoken language. Practitioners should be aware that robots such as Roamer, Pip and Pixie are not to be got out of the cupboard only when addressing mathematical development but should be accessible to children at all times.

The focus of this theme concerns making use of a simple word processor. *Clicker 4* (Crick Software) (Figure 4) is a good program to use because not only is it a talking word processor (always a bonus with young children) but it also has what are known as 'grids'. These are essentially on-screen word banks or a screen version of the overlays found on concept keyboards. Grids can be purchased for a variety of topics and there is actually a package called *Clicker 4 Nursery Rhymes* that could prove very useful when working on this particular theme. You can also find more grids, freely downloadable, suitable for this topic at the *LearningGrids* site (formerly known as CGfL – *Clicker Grids for Learning)* on the Web (**www.cricksoft.com/cgfl/uk/**).

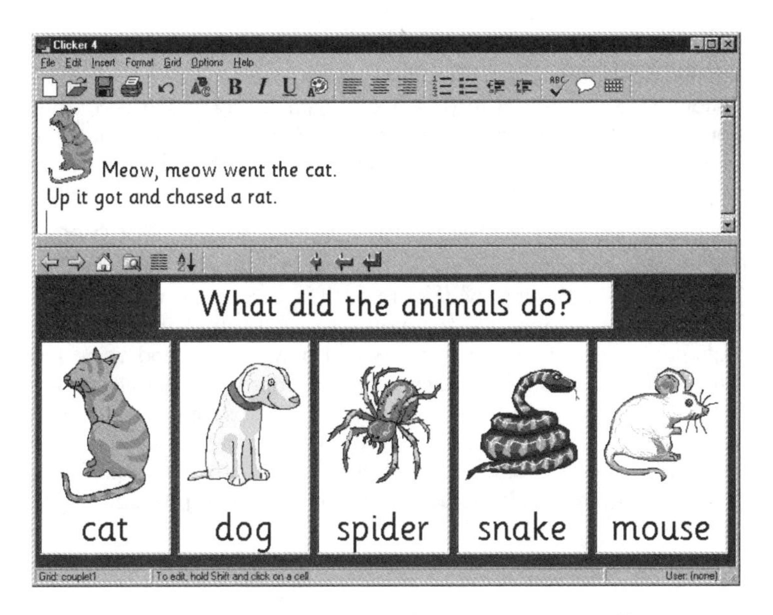

Figure 4 *Clicker 4* is great for creating text quickly

Grids can be created effortlessly by practitioners on whatever topic they choose. In this instance a grid facilitating the creation of invitations is needed. Pictures can be inserted as easily as text. Different versions of the same grid can be created to take into account the different abilities of the children. This sort of program is ideal for getting text on the screen quickly if keyboard skills, as well as reading and writing skills, are not sufficiently advanced. A few clicks of a mouse can lead to something quite startling, whereas 'hunt and peck' on the normal QWERTY keyboard can become a chore and quite demoralising.

However, we are most definitely not saying that a full-blown word-processing package, such as *Microsoft Word*, is of no use to the practitioner. Many children will enter the Foundation Stage quite familiar with this package as it is used so widely in the home. They will be happy to use the program and to show their less *au fait* peers what they can do. Whatever package is utilised the children will be enthralled by the fact that their prodding of the keyboard results in characters appearing on the monitor. Indeed, we would urge you to 'let them play'! Let them explore the keyboard and discover what happens. In the words of Cook and Finlayson (1999: p 10),

> *For young children, the word processor proves a delightful extension to other mark-making activities as they discover that holding down a key repeats the letter on the screen.*

An alternative to using a word processor is to use an e-mail program such as *Outlook Express*. The practitioner, using his or her own e-mail account, could pose as various characters from *The Jolly Postman*.

The children, with assistance from an adult, could e-mail invitations to Red Riding Hood, The Three Bears and so on. They could apply stationery to the e-mail to give it an invitation look and feel. They would, of course, ask for a response and imagine the excitement the next day when they access the e-mail program and find replies from those characters!

We feel we should say a few words about an enchanting CD-ROM that would seem ideal for use in this theme, namely, *The Jolly Post Office* (Dorling Kindersley) (Figure 5). It is, as are many of the CD-ROMs made especially for younger children, an engaging multimedia delight. However, we would only recommend using this with older, more able Foundation Stage children. The activities, even at the 'easy' level, are quite challenging, so the support of an adult becomes even more important. The facility to make your own invitations is one of the activities that could prove useful. Other areas of learning could be addressed by completing the remaining activities.

Figure 5 Practitioners could find *The Jolly Post Office* useful

MEDIUM-TERM PLAN

Area of learning	Learning objectives	Possible experiences	Resources
Communications, language and literacy	CCL 1: Enjoy listening to and responding to stories connected to *The Jolly Postman*	Listen to teacher reading *The Jolly Postman.* Follow this by using audio cassettes, CD-ROMs and websites to listen to fairy stories and nursery rhymes involving characters from the text	Cassette player Audio cassettes CD-ROMs Computer Internet access
	CCL: 2: Use language to imagine and recreate roles and experiences to retell some of the stories connected to *The Jolly Postman*	Record their own interpretation of famous stories and/or rhymes with a video recorder or audio cassette recorder	Video recorder TV Audio cassette recorder
	CCL 4: Know that print carries meaning and, in English, is read from left to right and top to bottom	Use websites that have nursery rhymes. Search and select the rhyme of choice, print and illustrate to make a class book	Printer Computer Internet access
	CCL 5: Attempt writing for different purposes, using features of different forms	• Use *Clicker 4* and a grid prepared by the practitioner to write a party invitation, inviting characters from the story • Use e-mail to send some party invitations	Printer Computer *Clicker 4* word-processing software E-mail software and account
	CCL 1: Interact with others, negotiating plans and activities and taking turns in conversation	In small groups program the *Roamer* (or other programmable robot) to deliver letters to characters in the story	*Roamer* (or other programmable toy)

SHORT-TERM PLAN

Focus	*The Jolly Postman*
Main area of learning	Communication, language and literacy
Learning objectives	CCL 5: Attempt writing for different purposes, using features of different forms
Prior learning	• Shared reading of *The Jolly Postman* and class discussion of the characters that enables the children to become familiar with them • Introduce children to the concept of 'an invitation' • Shared writing to model the layout of an invitation and key words to be used
Activity	• Practitioner to remind children of previous learning about invitations • Introduce the activity by telling children that they need to write an invitation because 'We're going to have a party and you can invite a character from the story' • Practitioner models how to use the *Clicker 4* software using the grid he or she prepared previously based on the children's contributions in the shared writing activity • Children work in pairs with adult support, to compose their invitation which includes graphics • Check, edit, save and print work
Resources	• Computer • *Clicker 4* talking word-processing software • Inkjet colour printer
Adult role	• Model and support appropriate ICT skills • Support children in identifying and using key words • Encourage children to proofread and/or to listen to the text being read by the program to ensure it makes sense • Support children in editing the text if necessary
ICT skills to be developed	• Use a simple word processor • Use of the mouse • Knowledge of how to save and print work
Assessment opportunities	• Can the child input text using the mouse and keyboard? • Can the child save and print work?
Follow-up activities	• Use a simple word-processing package to address envelopes to the characters using addresses from the story that have been prepared by the practitioner • Send e-mail invitations to characters – access the replies • Use the word processor to compose a shopping list of food to buy for the party
Links with other areas of learning	• PSED 3: Work as part of a group • PD 5: Handle tools and objects safely and with increasing control

6 Mathematical Development: 'Going Shopping'

The theme we have chosen for Mathematical Development is 'Going Shopping'. This is an excellent topic for aiding the development of important mathematical skills such as the use of mathematical language, number recognition, counting, addition and subtraction. There will also be opportunities for promoting data-handling skills, and for developing spatial awareness and directional language.

There has been an explosion in recent years of CD-ROMs aimed at the Foundation Stage market. Many of these are focused on developing the numeracy skills of Early Years children. Most of these have all the usual 'whistles and bells' that multimedia has to offer – sound effects, speech, colourful graphics, animations and video clips. All these engage the child and motivate in a way that may not be possible with other methods. These disks are made to be used independently although the presence of an adult is preferable to bring out the all-important 'maths talk'. Titles that may well be of use when covering this particular theme include *Percy's Money Box* (Neptune Computer), *Sum Shopping* (Cube Multimedia) and *SuperMarket* (Resource). The last two resources would be particularly appropriate for Reception children working in the daily mathematics lesson. There are many more CD-ROMs of the general mathematics type that could prove useful here, as well as others that aim at all-round skill development in numeracy, literacy and so on.

Many of these CD-ROMs are 'hosted' by the favourite TV characters of young children. This can only add motivational value. It is also the case with many websites too and, mirroring the growth in CD-ROMs aimed at the Foundation Stage, there has been a positive plethora of these springing up in recent years. Many are full-grown multimedia marvels like their CD-ROM counterparts but at a fraction of the cost. Of course, adult supervision is essential when children are using the internet. The Internet Service Providers (ISPs) for schools invariably offer a filtered service so that the 'web nasties' we've all heard and read about don't appear on the computer screen. However, these are not foolproof and the occasional story of something objectionable getting through is not unheard of. For more advice on being safe on the internet visit the Superhighway Safety site (**safety.ngfl.gov.uk/**).

Examples of websites suitable for this topic include *Loose Change Shopping Game* (**www.oup.co.uk/oxed/primary/funzone/funzone.html/omzshopping.html/**), *Moneykins* (**www.childrensmoneyworld.com/uk/menu/main.htm**) and *Money Talks* (**http://dfee.org/framework/r/money.html**). At its simplest level, *Toy Shop* (Figure 6) could prove useful. This program appears on the CD-ROM that comes with the DfES pack called *Using ICT to Support Mathematics in Primary Schools* and is also available for download from the standards site (**www.standards.dfee.gov.uk/numeracy/**). Educational games on the theme of money, appropriate for use in the Foundation Stage, can be found at *Teaching Money* (**www.teachingmoney.co.uk/**).

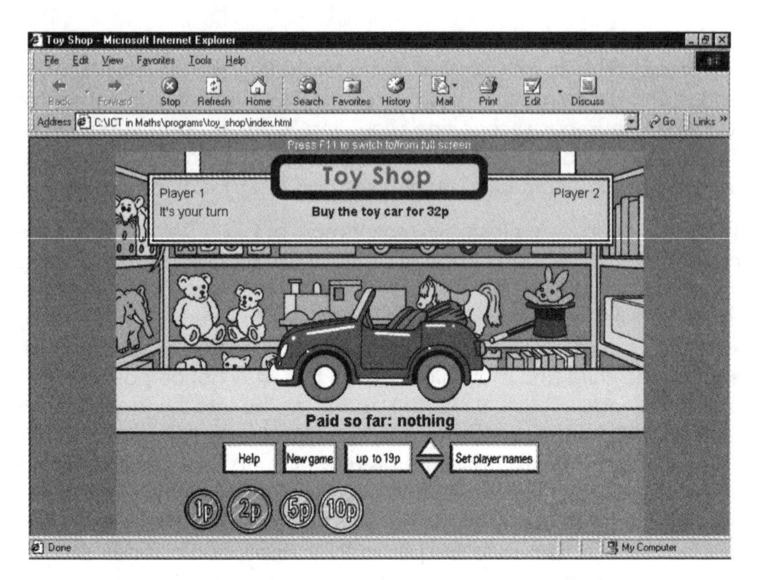

Figure 6 *Toy Shop* – get it from the web or from the DfES maths disk

For surveys a simple graphing package is needed. There are many programs to be found that fit this description. We recommend *Starting Graph* (RM) and *Counter for Windows* (Black Cat) (Figure 7) but there are numerous others we could mention. *PicturePoint* (Longman Logotron) has an added bonus in that the graphs produced speak! Using this type of software will build up the children's data-handling skills and help them to recognise patterns in data and make logical deductions. The children collect the data, perhaps using a data-collection sheet produced by, or preferably, *with* their teacher, and take it across to the computer. The program will have been modelled to the class previously but adult assistance should be available so that they can enter the data, quickly produce a graph (usually a pictogram, block graph or bar chart) and then get on to the important business of interpreting their findings.

Other software for the delivery of this theme includes a graphics program to view, edit and print pictures taken on a visit to a supermarket. An investigation of shape (based on products seen) could include work with a simple painting program. This could even be done with a word processor or desktop publisher these days using a 'shape tool'. The framework software *My World 3* (Inclusive Technology) might prove very useful too, having 'screens' available on maths-related topics for the Foundation Stage. The word-

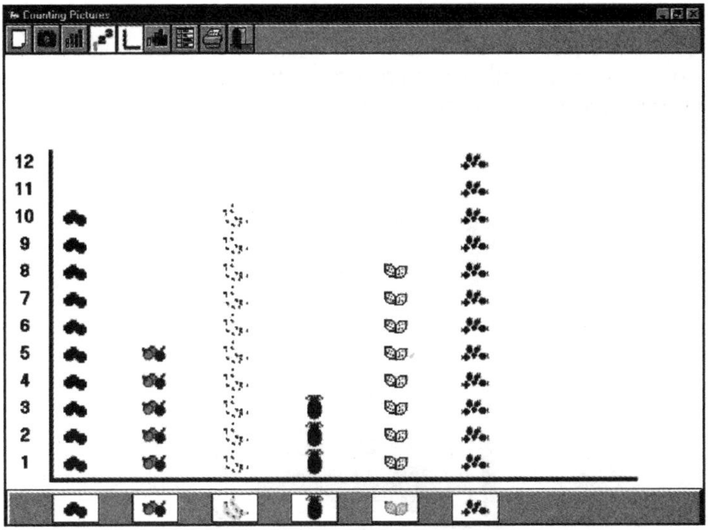

Figure 7 *Counting Pictures* (part of *Counter for Windows*)

processor *Clicker 4* will be ideal for printing out shopping lists and price lists (complete with pictures!) for the role-play area. A grid, prepared by the practitioner, could be used to make the computer (and printer) a shopping till. However, it should be noted that toy electronic cash registers are available (from certain toy shops or educational suppliers) and these will make things more realistic. The keypad will be much like that of a calculator and will only aid the development of number skills.

In the words of Avril Loveless (1995, p78):

> *Control technology offers the opportunity for an investigative approach to solving problems and development in the complexity of giving and modifying instructions.*

The focus for this topic is making use of a programmable toy. We mention using the *Roamer* (Valiant Technology) (Figure 8) but any suitable robot will do.

Figure 8 The *Roamer*

New directional toys are appearing in shops all the time these days and at the right price too! *The Ladybug* (TTNS) is one such with its colourful design and a simple, five-button keypad. *Pip* and *Pixie* (Swallow Systems) are very good too and well established in schools. *Pixie* is especially appropriate for young children as it has a very simple, straightforward keypad (see Figure 9).

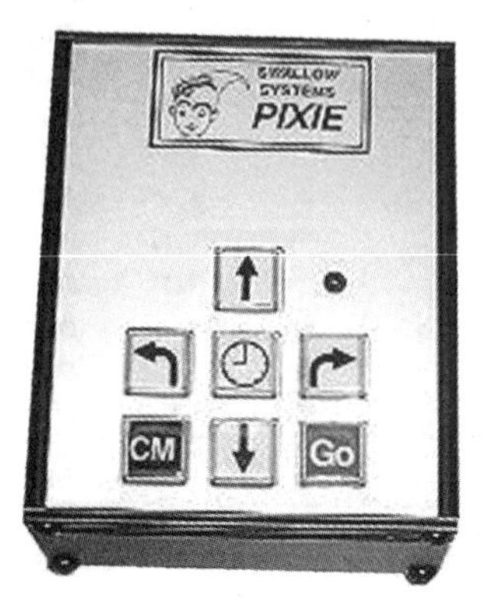

Figure 9 The *Pixie*

A mat for the floor robot to travel around is a good idea (Figure 10). These can be prepared by the practitioner or bought from the producers of the robot; many different ones are available these days. Plastic covers for the *Roamer* can be purchased and these can be used to 'dress up' the robot so that it looks like a character (in this case it could be a car or even a person) and is given some personality. This makes it all the more meaningful to the children.

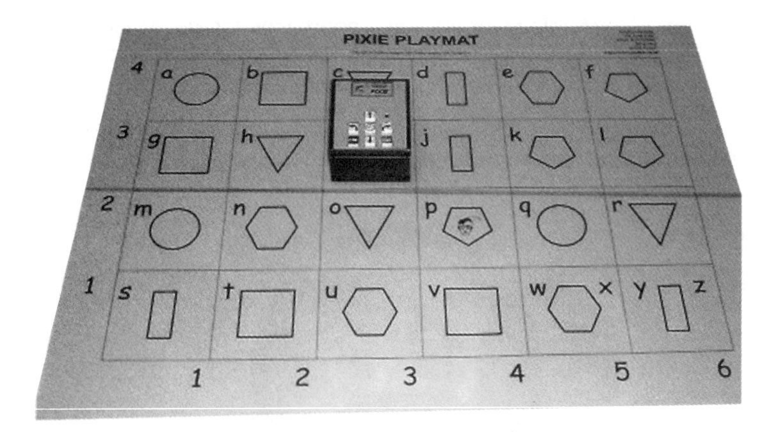

Figure 10 A playmat for *Pixie*

The benefits language-wise of using these toys have been discussed in the last chapter but the maths-specific language promoted by their use should not be underestimated. Instructional language in particular is developed because the robot will not move until it has been programmed. Number skills are promoted because a numerical input is required to specify how far you want the robot to travel, wait and turn. Concepts such as number recognition, number value, direction, angle, shape and space are all fostered by using a robot such as the *Roamer*. For a fuller list of the *Roamer*'s pedagogical advantages, see the article by Donahue on the Valiant website (**www.valiant-technology.com**).

Once children are secure in using a floor robot they can graduate to using a 'screen turtle' in one of the many versions of Logo available. The *2go* program, which is part of *Infant Video Toolbox,* is a simple way to start (Figure 11).

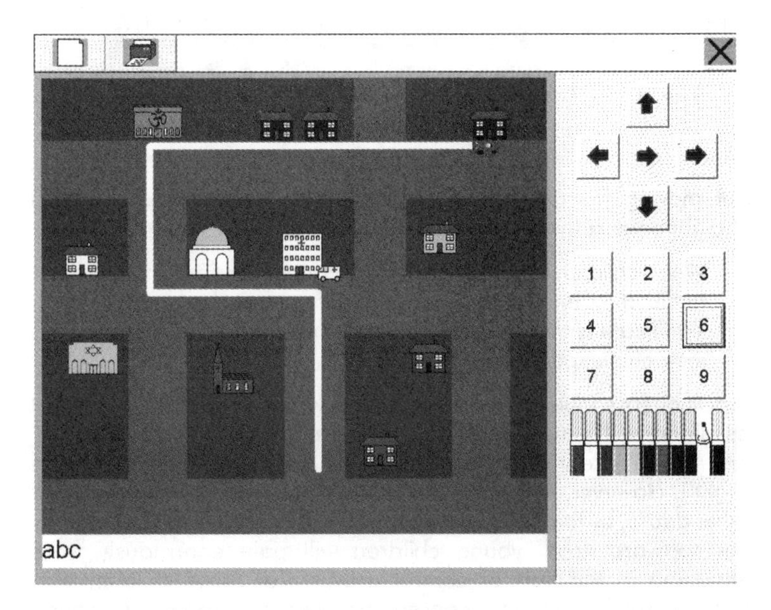

Figure 11 2go is a simple way to start using a 'screen turtle'

We are fond of *RoamerWorld* (RM) (Figure 12), which uses the same interface as the *Roamer* itself and has a 'shopping' background ('Birthday Present') to explore. This way we are building in continuity and progression. The interface (keypad) may be the same but the children are dealing with a more abstract 2-D object moving across a computer screen, rather than a concrete 3-D object moving along the floor.

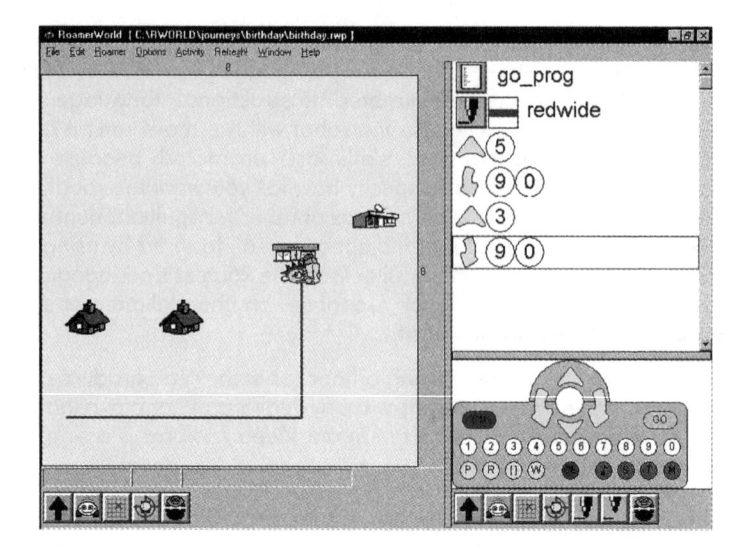

Figure 12 *RoamerWorld* – a good way to introduce the idea of the screen turtle

But moving from the 'floor turtle' to the 'screen turtle' is not a straightforward matter. As Helen Smith (1999, p37) puts it:

> *When children first move from the* Roamer *or* Pixie *to the screen turtle, they encounter important differences. Perhaps the most significant is that the screen turtle moves in a vertical plane. This may challenge spatial thinking.*

Practitioners should be aware that there will be problems here. Adult assistance will be needed as children get to grips with the fact that 'up' and 'down' are in fact 'forward' or 'backward' (or even 'left' and 'right'). However, with the right scaffolding by the practitioner and other adults, by the more knowledgeable peers of the children and by the software itself, young children will gain enormously from engaging in this sort of control activity. For those children who really struggle with this concept use two programs, *Strawberry Garden* and *Unit the Robot*, both on the DfES disk *Using ICT to Support Mathematics in the Primary School*.

MEDIUM-TERM PLAN

Area of learning	Learning objectives	Possible experiences	Resources
Mathematical Development	MD 1: Say and use number names in shopping activities Count reliably up to 10 in shopping activities Recognise numerals from 1 to 9 Use developing mathematical ideas and methods to solve practical problems MD 2: In practical activities begin to use vocabulary and language related to addition and subtraction	• Children will use a variety of mathematics software, CD-ROMs and websites to develop number skills such as labelling, counting and calculating • Use a simple graphing program to conduct surveys about favourite products • Use an electronic cash register in a role-play situation to buy and sell goods • Use a simple word-processing program to make price tags for goods on sale • Use *Clicker 4* to create pictorial price lists for display in the 'shop'	Mathematics CD-ROMs such as *Supermarket* (Resource), *Percy's Money Box* (Neptune Computer) Computer Commercially produced electronic cash register toy Simple graphing processor (e.g. *Counting Pictures*) Simple word processor (e.g. *Clicker 4*) Printer Internet access
	MD 3: Use everyday words to describe position	Program the *Roamer* (or other programmable toy) to go on a shopping trip. This could be on a specially prepared mat or around the classroom	*Roamer* (or other programmable toy)
	MD 3: Use language such as 'greater', 'smaller', 'heavier' or 'lighter' to compare quantities	• Use digital camera whilst on a class visit to the supermarket to record shapes, sizes, weights and quantities of products • Download pictures to the computer, print out for display and discuss in relation to the relevant mathematical language	Computer Graphics software Printer Digital camera

SHORT-TERM PLAN

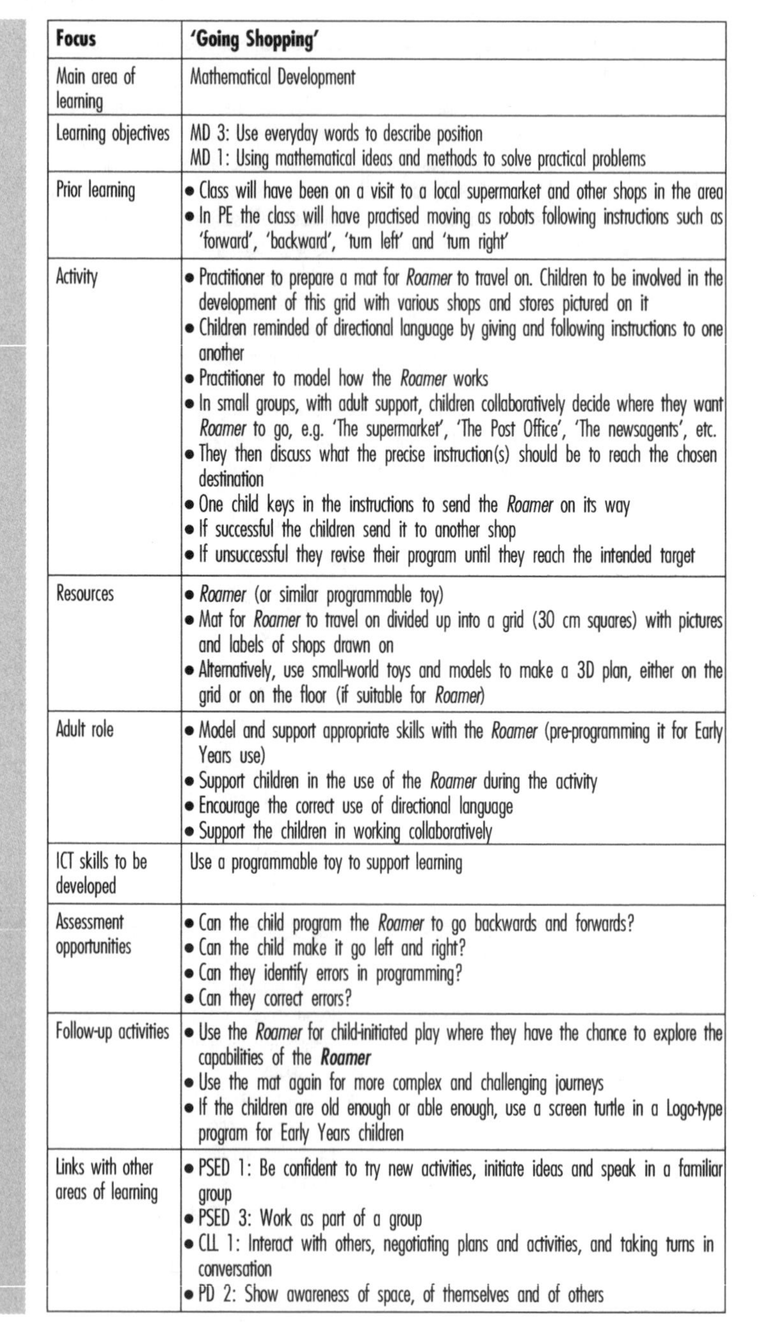

Focus	**'Going Shopping'**
Main area of learning	Mathematical Development
Learning objectives	MD 3: Use everyday words to describe position MD 1: Using mathematical ideas and methods to solve practical problems
Prior learning	• Class will have been on a visit to a local supermarket and other shops in the area • In PE the class will have practised moving as robots following instructions such as 'forward', 'backward', 'turn left' and 'turn right'
Activity	• Practitioner to prepare a mat for *Roamer* to travel on. Children to be involved in the development of this grid with various shops and stores pictured on it • Children reminded of directional language by giving and following instructions to one another • Practitioner to model how the *Roamer* works • In small groups, with adult support, children collaboratively decide where they want *Roamer* to go, e.g. 'The supermarket', 'The Post Office', 'The newsagents', etc. • They then discuss what the precise instruction(s) should be to reach the chosen destination • One child keys in the instructions to send the *Roamer* on its way • If successful the children send it to another shop • If unsuccessful they revise their program until they reach the intended target
Resources	• *Roamer* (or similar programmable toy) • Mat for *Roamer* to travel on divided up into a grid (30 cm squares) with pictures and labels of shops drawn on • Alternatively, use small-world toys and models to make a 3D plan, either on the grid or on the floor (if suitable for *Roamer*)
Adult role	• Model and support appropriate skills with the *Roamer* (pre-programming it for Early Years use) • Support children in the use of the *Roamer* during the activity • Encourage the correct use of directional language • Support the children in working collaboratively
ICT skills to be developed	Use a programmable toy to support learning
Assessment opportunities	• Can the child program the *Roamer* to go backwards and forwards? • Can the child make it go left and right? • Can they identify errors in programming? • Can they correct errors?
Follow-up activities	• Use the *Roamer* for child-initiated play where they have the chance to explore the capabilities of the ***Roamer*** • Use the mat again for more complex and challenging journeys • If the children are old enough or able enough, use a screen turtle in a Logo-type program for Early Years children
Links with other areas of learning	• PSED 1: Be confident to try new activities, initiate ideas and speak in a familiar group • PSED 3: Work as part of a group • CLL 1: Interact with others, negotiating plans and activities, and taking turns in conversation • PD 2: Show awareness of space, of themselves and of others

7 Personal, Social and Emotional Development: 'All About Me'

'All About Me' is always a popular theme with young children. It is often suggested as a topic under the Physical Development heading but we suggest it as one that could be covered under the Personal, Social and Emotional Development area of learning. The theme relies heavily on children being able to bring in materials, photographs, books and artefacts related to their lives at home. In today's *You've Been Framed!* age, children should also be able to bring videos to share their experiences with others in the class. From these stimuli much oral, written and pictorial work will follow.

This topic focuses more on issues such as family, friends, pets, culture and special occasions. It will give children the opportunity to see different lifestyles in their own culture and that of others, particularly in a multiethnic era. Therefore the use of CD-ROMs such as *Here I Am* (Cambridgeshire Software House), *All About Ourselves* (SEMERC) (Figure 13) and *All About Me* (Dorling Kindersley), though they sound appropriate, may not be suitable in this context. On the other hand, however, there may well be sections on the titles that fit the bill nicely. Practitioners must decide whether their use is fitting.

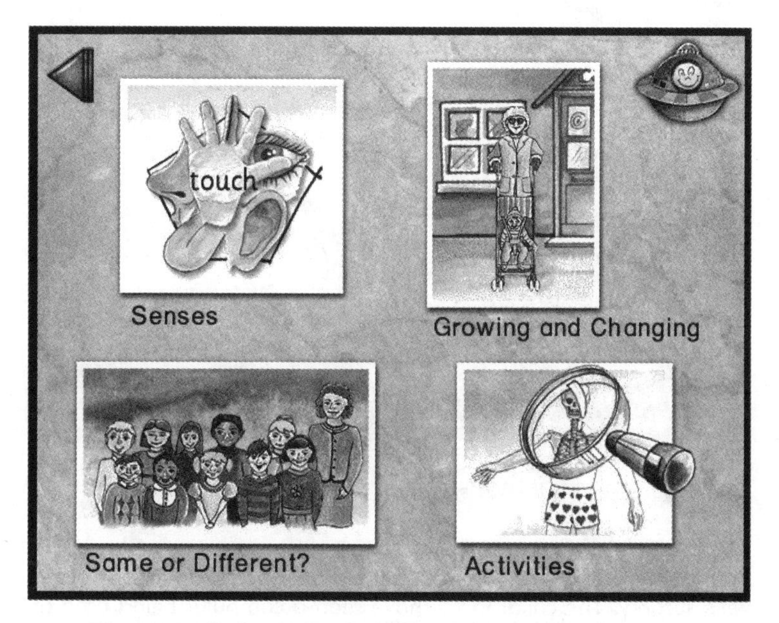

Figure 13 *All About Ourselves* – could be useful in this topic

Various ICT devices will be needed during the course of this theme and the children themselves can be given the opportunity to operate the equipment – after all, they probably do so at home! Practitioners should bear this in mind when using the television, video player, digital camera, computer, printer and scanner. Of course, given the 'digital divide', some children may be in need of practice in the operation of certain pieces of ICT equipment and practitioners should see that they get it. However, whether competent users or not, the children should be supervised by an adult in the interests of safety, not to mention the financial considerations of misuse!

Use can be made once more of the word processor for providing labels and captions. It will be another opportunity to improve mouse skills and gain familiarity with the keyboard. Use will also be made of the internet, in particular a government website for young children called *Welltown* (**www.welltown.gov.uk/**) that looks at PSHE. This site will be covered in more depth in the next chapter. Suffice to say, however, that it will be useful in this particular instance for learning about safety. Also, don't miss the section entitled 'Me and My Family'.

The focus for this particular theme is to make a role-play area after a visit to the vet's. Children will also be making use of the CD-ROM called *At the Vet's* (Granada) (Figure 14).

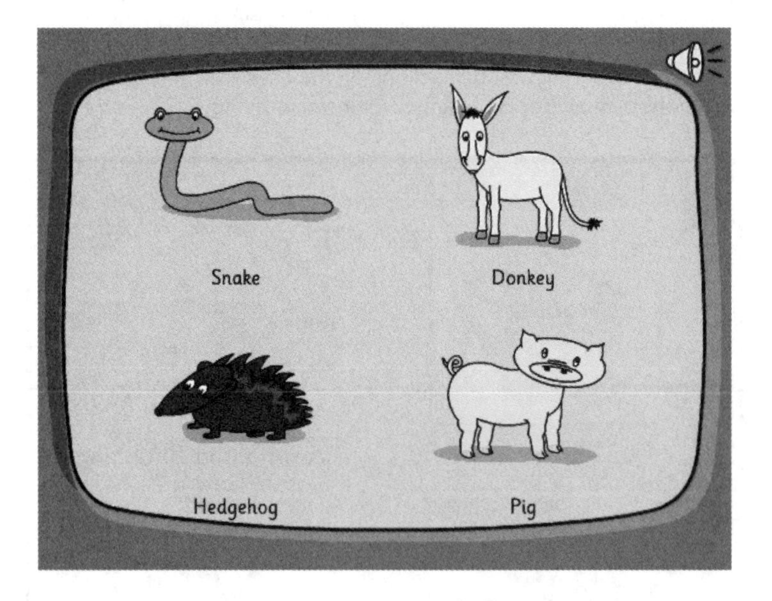

Figure 14 *At the Vet's* – which pet are you bringing today?

This is one title in a series that is designed to support role play in the Foundation Stage. The role-play area should be set up to look like a vet's surgery. The children will have seen a computer being used at the vet's on a previous visit and they too can use it, through the program, to take patient and pet details, enter information about symptoms and treatments, and print out prescriptions and bills. A range of pets can be brought into the surgery. Medicine can be taken out of cupboards and safely locked away. Stethoscopes and X-ray machines can be used to make diagnoses. All this fosters creative play where 'real life' is imitated. Like so many CD-ROMs these days this one comes complete with teacher's notes and printable resources including simple worksheets for the children. This bright, colourful, engaging package makes children take responsibility for their own learning and its sound prompts and general simplicity should help even the shyest child to grow in confidence.

Other software and hardware could be used in this role-play scenario. A word processor, perhaps using an appropriate grid in *Clicker 4*, might be used to create price lists (with pictures). Posters might be designed and printed using a paint program or DTP software. Searches for pictures of animals could be carried out on the internet using Google Image Search (**www.google.com/imghp**). These could then be printed or downloaded for inclusion in documents. The electronic cash register could be used again in this situation. All this adds to the realism of the setting. It develops awareness of everyday technology and ICT. This is exactly the kind of classroom activity whereby young children, as Cook and Finlayson (1999) observed, are not only learning *about* ICT but learning *through* it as well.

Example medium- and short-term plans for the theme of 'All about me' can be seen on pages 54 and 55.

MEDIUM-TERM PLAN

Area of learning	Learning objectives	Possible experiences	Resources
Personal, Social and Emotional Development	PSED 2: Have a developing awareness of their own needs, views and feelings and be sensitive to those of others Have a developing respect for their own cultures and beliefs and those of others	• Use videos and photographs to talk about and share features of their own family life and culture • Children create an 'All About Me' book. Photographs of family members (including pets) can be scanned into the computer. These can then be labelled and captions can be added using a simple word processor	Computer Scanner Simple word processor Printer Video player TV
	PSED 2: Respond to significant experiences, showing a range of feelings when appropriate PSED 6: Understand that people have different needs, views, cultures and beliefs, that need to be treated with respect Understand that they can expect others to treat their needs, views, cultures and beliefs with respect	• Extend previous work on the 'All About Me' books by focusing on special occasions and events. Use photographs, videos and books to help understand and respect the unique culture and beliefs of each family • Special artefacts can brought into the classroom by the children and these can be photographed with a digital camera for inclusion in the child's book and for display purposes	Computer Scanner Simple word processor Printer Video player Digital camera
	PSED 4: Understand what is right, what is wrong, and why. Consider the consequences of their words and actions for themselves and others	• Use the Welltown website (**www.welltown.gov.uk/teachers/sitemap.html**) to explore making choices and the consequences of their actions. With adult support the 'Am I Safe?' and 'Be Safe in the Sun' sections may be of particular use. NB: This site will also be helpful when looking at the family	Computer Internet access
	PSED 1: Continue to be interested, excited and movitated to learn. Be confident to try new activities, initiate ideas and speak in a familiar group PSED 3: Form good relationships with adults and peers. Work as part of a group or class taking turns and sharing fairly	Following a visit to a local veterinary surgery set up a role-play area as 'The Vets'. Use the *At the Vet's* CD-ROM (Brilliant Computing) to enable the children to be a vet, to take patient details, diagnose the problem and prescribe treatment	Computer CD-ROM *At the Vet's*

SHORT-TERM PLAN

Focus	'All About Me'
Main area of learning	Personal, Social and Emotional Development
Learning objectives	PSED 1: Continue to be interested, excited and motivated to learn. Be confident to try new activities, initiate ideas and speak in a familiar group. Form good relationships with adults and peers PSED 3: Work as part of a group or class taking turns and sharing fairly
Prior learning	• Class will have talked about their own pets during the making of their own 'All About Me' book which may well include photographs of their pet • The class will have visited a real veterinary surgery to gain an understanding of the purpose of a vet and how animals are cared for. They will have been made aware of the real-life uses of ICT
Activity	• Recall and discuss their visit to 'the Vet's' • The children will help to design and plan their own veterinary surgery including ICT devices needed, e.g. computer, telephone, printer, cash register, etc. • Practitioner models how to use the *At the Vet's* program whilst playing in role with the children • This should then develop into a child-initiated activity where children have regular opportunities to revisit and play independently with sensitive and appropriate adult intervention
Resources	• Computer, *At the Vet's* CD-ROM, printer, telephone, cash register • Appropriate dressing-up clothes and props (including a range of 'pets', e.g. cuddly toys, plastic reptiles, etc.)
Adult role	• Model and support appropriate skills with the CD-ROM • Participate in children's play when appropriate • Support sensitively children in problem-solving and resolving difficulties
ICT skills to be developed	• Continued development of mouse skills • Awareness and understanding of everyday uses of ICT
Assessment opportunities	• Can the child use the mouse to navigate the program and select the correct item? • Can children use other ICT equipment to facilitate their play?
Follow-up activities	• Access and use the teacher support material (activity sheets) on the *At the Vet's* CD-ROM as extension activities • Access the internet to find and print pictures of animals for display in the 'waiting room' • Use a simple word processor (perhaps *Clicker 4* with a grid prepared by the practitioner) to make a price list of things on sale at the vet's
Links with other areas of learning	• CLL 1: Interact with others, negotiating plans and activities, and taking turns in conversation • MD 1: Count and use number names in familiar contexts • KUW 3: Find out about and identify the uses of everyday technology and use ICT to support learning • CD 3: Use imagination in role play

8 Physical Development: 'Let's Move!'

'Let's Move!' is our theme in the Physical Development area of learning. This topic focuses on children responding, through movement and dance, to songs, rhymes and rhythms. As an extension to this, they will look at what happens to their bodies when they exert themselves. As the theme is concerned with movement and spatial awareness we also take this opportunity to develop the mouse and keyboard skills of the children. Perhaps this is reason enough to cover this particular theme at the beginning of the school year.

Many of the examples included in previous chapters will improve the mouse control skills of the children – this is a by-product of most computer-based activities these days. Young children, even as young as 2 or 3 years old, soon come to realise that the pointer on the screen corresponds to their movements of the mouse. One of the Stepping Stones in the Foundation Stage guidance specifies that children should 'use one-handed tools and equipment' (p 114). The mouse is probably the most commonly used one-handed tool in today's world. It seems only right that they should learn to master it as soon as possible if they are to access all the benefits ICT has to offer.

A mouse specifically designed for small hands is a must for the Early Years setting. Granada's 'mini-mouse' that flashes when clicked is a good choice. Berchet Media's 'Mouse for Tiny Tots' is an alternative option and comes with a CD-ROM containing five activities aimed at developing mouse skills in young children. Practitioners are reminded that in Windows it is easy to change the size of the mouse pointer, the mouse speed and the double-click speed. There are, of course, plenty of software packages on the market with a similar aim. *My World* 'screens' will certainly be of use here – the classic 'dress teddy' exercise springs to mind (Figure 15). Games like 'Jigsaw' and 'Sheep' in *Tizzy's Toybox* (Sherston) (Figure 16) will also help.

Learn PC: Mouse and Keyboard Skills (Neptune Computer) is designed for 3-year-olds and upwards and should prove beneficial. There are also websites aplenty suitable for this particular activity out there in cyberspace if you are prepared to look. A brief browse around the net led to us finding *CBeebies Click-a-pic!* (**www.bbc.co.uk/cbeebies/funandgames/clickapics/index.shtml**), *Early Mouse Skills* (**ngfl.northumberland.gov.uk/ict/mouseskills/Default.htm**) and *Tidy the Classroom* (**www.bgfl.org/bgfl/activities/intranet/ks1/ict/mouse/index.htm**).

> *Some schools have found that, if basic keyboard skills are taught at an early stage, then confidence and ease of use of the computer have a positive effect on the child's work throughout the curriculum.*
>
> (BECTa, 2001)

Figure 15 'Dress Teddy' – a classic *My World* exercise

Figure 16 'Jigsaw' – an activity in *Tizzy's Toybox*

Keyboard skills, though secondary to mouse skills at this stage, will become more important as children progress through the Foundation Stage. A growing awareness of the layout and general functionality of the traditional QWERTY keyboard is to be encouraged. The importance of keys such as SHIFT, SPACE BAR and ENTER should be gradually introduced as the children are ready. Concept (or overlay) keyboards can be used at first. These can also be used in tandem with the normal keyboard. Lower-case keyboards are available, as are sets of stickers that cover upper-case letters on the keyboard. This will not only help children to become familiar with the keyboard but aid the development of letter recognition as well. Investing in a game such as *Keyboard Crazy* (Keywise Systems) could bring benefits. This innovative new game has, apparently, led to a marked improvement in children's keyboard skills according to the results from a pilot scheme. Software titles such as *Jump Ahead Typing* (Random House) and online typing tutors on the web may also be of use.

Once again music cassettes and CDs are going to be very useful in this topic. Websites too might be worth visiting to access words and music to 'action songs' such as 'A Sailor Went to Sea', 'Heads, Shoulders, Knees and Toes' and 'Everybody Do This'. These, and many more, can be viewed on the *Tweenies Song Time* web page (**www.bbc.co.uk/cbeebies/tweenies/songtime/**) (Figure 17).

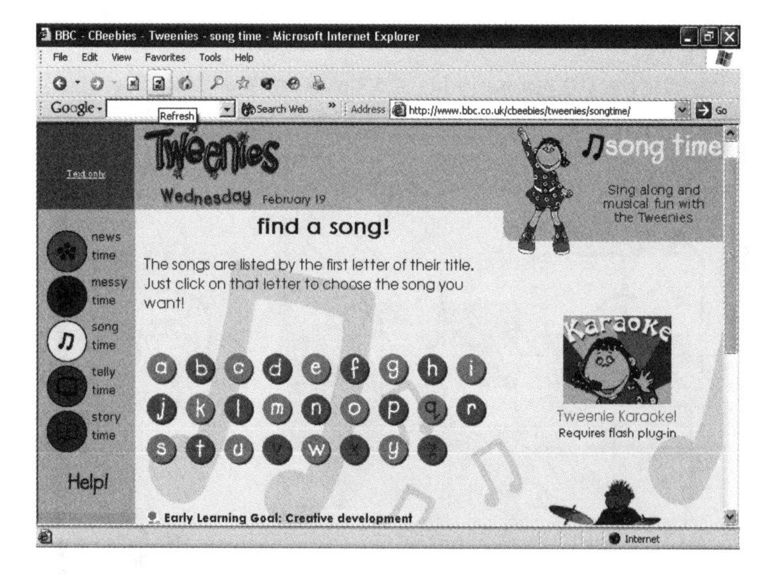

Figure 17 The *Tweenies Song Time* web page

A video camera could be used to record the children performing. Their efforts could then be watched on a TV screen, much to their delight no doubt. Use could once more be made of programmable toys. After they have followed instructions for moving, perhaps acting as 'robots' themselves, they could go on to make the floor robot move forward and backward, turn right and left. They could even move with them in a 'follow the leader' type game.

The focused activity of this particular theme is use of the internet, specifically the previously mentioned *Welltown* website. As will be obvious from reading previous chapters in this book, we are big fans of the internet. It offers so many opportunities and possibilities, both to the children in their learning, and to practitioners in their wider professional role. Some may be doubtful of its worth but many children, even at the Foundation Stage, will be used to using various child-friendly websites at home. In a newspaper article by Stephen Hoare (2002), a BECTa Early Years' adviser was asked: 'When is it appropriate to introduce children to the internet?' Her reply was unequivocal:

> *As soon as they are ready. Introduction to the internet at the Foundation Stage is desirable so long as it is done correctly. It's a similar issue to the question 'How soon shall I start children reading?' The answer is – as soon as they're ready.*

Given the recognised dangers of the internet practitioners should always ensure that children are supervised by an adult when using websites. An 'acceptable use policy' should be in place whereby parents are made fully aware of how the web is used. This policy should be adhered to at all times. Of course, web pages can be downloaded to hard disks prior to their use and the need to go online is negated.

The *Welltown* website (Figure 18) will allow children to find out about healthy eating so that they have healthy bodies for all those exciting 'moving' activities. Once there they can visit the 'dining hall' and play the 'Food Game'. The children can then go to the 'playground' and find out about games of different kinds. These can be printed out and later tried in their own playground. Practitioners will find the 'Teachers and Parents' page useful.

Figure 18 The *Welltown* website

MEDIUM-TERM PLAN

Area of learning	Learning objectives	Possible experiences	Resources
Physical Development	PD 1: Move with confidence, imagination and in safety Move with control and coordination PD 2: Show awareness of space, of themselves and of others	• Use cassette tapes and audio CDs to play music to move to • Use websites and CD-ROMs to search for 'action' songs and respond to them • Use a video camera to record the children performing	Cassette player and appropriate music cassettes CD player and appropriate music CDs Websites/CD-ROMs featuring action songs Video camera (with tripod if possible) Computer Internet access CD-ROMs
	PD 4: Use a range of small and large equipment PD 5: Handle tools and objects...with increasing control	• Use a range of websites/CD-ROMs to practise and develop mouse skills • Use CD-ROMs to practise and develop keyboard skills	Computer Internet access CD-ROMs
	PD 2: Show awareness of space, of themselves and of others	• Use a remote-control toy to manoeuvre around the classroom • Program a floor robot (e.g. *Pixie* or *Roamer*) to send it to a partner taking account of the space available, other children and furniture	Remote-control toy *Roamer*(s) *Pixie*(s)
	PD 3: Recognise the importance of keeping healthy and those things which contribute to this. Recognise the changes that happen to their bodies when they are active	• Use the *Welltown* website and visit the school (inside and outside) to find out about healthy eating and things to do to be active • Use CD-ROMs to find out about what happens to the body when it is active	Computer Internet access CD-ROMs

SHORT-TERM PLAN

Focus	'Let's Move!'
Main area of learning	Physical Development
Learning objectives	PD 3: Recognise the importance of keeping healthy and those things which contribute to this. Recognise the changes that happen to their bodies when they are active
Prior learning	• Children will have talked about the importance of being active and eating healthy foods • They will share their own understanding and experiences of how they keep healthy • Children should be competent in using a mouse
Activity	• Explain to the children that we are going to use the internet to find out how to keep healthy • Ask them what sort of information we might find • Introduce them to the *Welltown* site and provide support when necessary • Children can visit the dining hall and play the 'Food game' • Children can also visit the playground, find out about active games and print them out • These can be used as a reference when playing outside
Resources	• Computer • Internet access • Printer
Adult role	• Be sensitive in acknowledging that there will be some things with regard to being healthy that will be out of the children's control • Be present whenever children are using the internet • Support children's learning through modelling, questioning and guiding when appropriate
ICT skills to be developed	• Know how to log on to the internet and load the browser • Know how to navigate around websites via hyperlinks and buttons
Assessment opportunities	• Can the child find the information required? • Can the child print out information once found?
Follow-up activities	• Use the printed information to play games outside (or in the hall) • Talk about the changes that happen to their bodies when active
Links with other areas of learning	• PSED 5: Dress and undress independently and manage their own personal hygiene • CLL 1: Interact with others, negotiating plans and activities and taking turns in conversation • KUW 1: Ask questions about why things happen and how things work

9 Creative Development: 'Stars and Moons'

Our final theme is in the Creative Development area of learning and, through our 'Stars and Moons' topic, explores ways of developing the skills of budding artists and musicians. Once more the use of music cassettes and CDs will be to the fore, as will the internet and CD-ROMs. These have been discussed at some length previously. However, music software and paint programs have not.

ICT can be very helpful when doing musical activities. It can:

- introduce children to a wide variety of musical styles;
- allow children to investigate and control sounds and structures;
- aid children in composing their own tunes;
- provide resources for learning the words to songs;
- provide accompaniment to movement, dance and performances;
- provide a means of recording performances;
- assist children in learning about musical instruments and the sounds they make.

Many of the ICT resources necessary to achieve this have already been mentioned – music cassettes, CDs, websites and CD-ROMs. However, there are software packages available, suitable for use by the Early Years child, which the practitioner would do well to consider. These allow the children to explore sounds and to make their own compositions. Of course, no one is suggesting that using actual musical instruments is not preferable but these are not always available in the Early Years setting. Besides which, ICT can help younger children to 'find a way in' to what can be a difficult area of learning. Furthermore, as Potter (2002, p 124) puts it,

> *Children learn that computers are capable of storing more than text and images but that they can be used to record and manipulate sound. To put it another way, they learn that sound itself can be represented and stored digitally in which form it can be transformed in many different ways.*

There are a number of music packages on the market that are worth consideration when deciding which one to purchase. *Beetles* (Brilliant) (Figure 19) is a delight. The animated insects can be given a musical instrument to play and then a song is chosen for them to perform. Various combinations can be tried. The children have to choose the most appropriate instrument(s) for a particular song.

Figure 19 *Beetles* – a lovely way to explore music

MusicMaker 1 (Resource) with its cassette recorder-like controls allows young children to take the first steps along the road to understanding musical concepts. Tunes can be composed, recorded and played back. *Compose World Junior* (ESP) is another music exploration package where musical phrases are represented by pictures.

All these programs are of the entertaining (not to say 'edutaining') multimedia type. They will engage and motivate the child and, where composition is involved, enable the learner to be seen as what Scrimshaw (1997) calls a 'creator'. They will also help to develop crucial listening skills. Websites that offer a similar experience include *The Amblephone* and *The Rodent Choir* (**ambleweb.digitalbrain.com/ambleweb/web/Games/?verb=view**), *CBeebies Music Game* (**www.bbc.co.uk/cbeebies/funandgames/index4.shtml**) and *Alfy's Music Mania* (**www.alfy.com/Music_Mania/index1.asp?FlashDetect=True**).

The focus for this area of learning is making use of a paint program. Young children always find these fascinating and there are many excellent packages around today for the Foundation Stage that are simple but powerful tools. According to BECTa, such a program can enhance the Early Years curriculum in the following ways.

- It allows exploration of sequences of actions and links between events and actions (e.g. what are the consequences of using this tool? If I move the mouse this way what happens?).
- It allows young children to incorporate elements into drawings that they would not be capable of producing with traditional materials (e.g. they can draw perfectly round circles).

- It allows children to experiment with new creative tools some of which are unique to ICT (e.g. rainbow paint, shape tools).
- It gives children access to tools which emulate existing techniques (e.g. spray paint or water brush).
- Children can try out things to see 'what would happen if'. They can easily undo, rub out or start again to make changes.

There are numerous marvellous paint packages we could mention here. Some of our favourites include *Colour Magic* (RM), *Kidpix Studio Deluxe* (Learning Company) (Figure 20), *Dazzle* (SEMERC) and *2Paint* (part of 2Simple's *Infant Video Toolbox*). There are many more worthy contenders and even *Paint*, the basic art program that comes with Microsoft Windows, is worth using if you have no alternative. All these packages come with a paint palette and the same basic tools – draw, brush, line, fill, shape, text, rubber, save and print. Some have extras such as ready-made backgrounds and 'stamps'. Some even have sound effects as tools are used just to add to the 'Wow!' factor. These tools make it easy to create something to be proud of.

Figure 20 Picture created in *Kidpix Studio* using the fill, shape, stamp and text tools

The practitioner will need to be fully familiar with the package and the various tools. This goes without saying really. If a teacher is not *au fait* with a program how can he or she model it properly? With all software a certain level of competence and confidence is required but this is especially the case with paint packages. Naturally the children will wish to print off their masterpieces so a colour printer is essential. These are relatively cheap to buy nowadays and are very worthwhile given the amount of satisfaction and increased self-esteem when on-screen efforts become 'hard copy'.

Of course, use could be made of a desktop publishing (DTP) program or even a word processor, which now tend to be full-featured DTP packages in their own right. They contain many of the tools common to graphics programs – line, shape, fill and (obviously!) text. 'Fuzzy-felt' style exercises could be prepared by the practitioner which involve 'dragging and dropping' stars and moons into the drawing area on screen. Using a 'copy' tool a wrapping-paper effect could be achieved by repeating a pattern.

There are websites that allow children to create pictures online. In the past this type of site has been notoriously slow but things have improved. Web technology has developed and with the advent of broadband connections for schools 'www' no longer has to mean 'World Wide Wait'! One of the best examples we've seen is *Artbox* (Figure 21) on the *CBeebies* website (**www.bbc.co.uk/cbeebies/artbox/**). This beautiful website offers a whole range of art activities and also gives children the option of sending their work to the *CBeebies Art Gallery*. Posting children's work around the classroom is always good for their self-esteem but showcasing their work on the internet, where it can be appreciated by a global audience, takes it to another level. Just imagine the excitement generated!

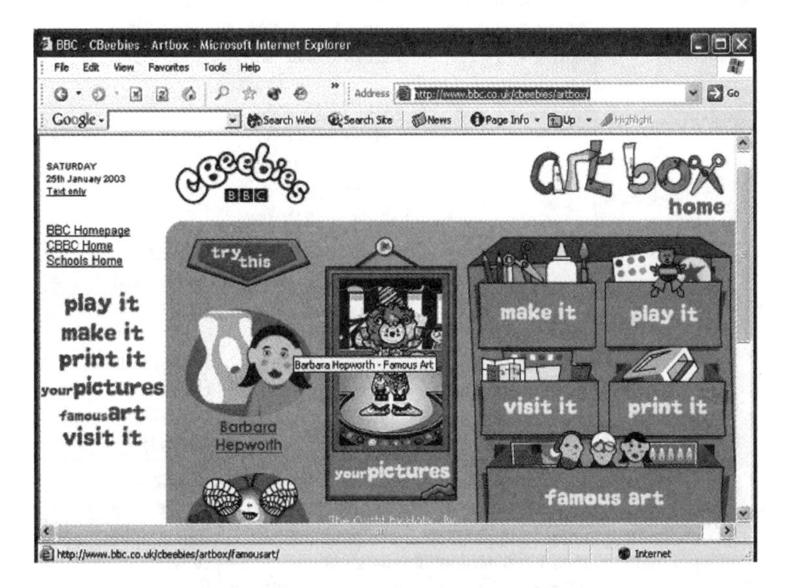

Figure 21 The amazing *Artbox* website

MEDIUM-TERM PLAN

Area of learning	Learning objectives	Possible experiences	Resources
Creative Development	CD 1: Explore colour, texture, shape, form and space in two or three dimensions	• Use a simple painting package (e.g. *2Paint, Dazzle, Kidpix*) to explore how to draw stars, moons and other 'night time' shapes • Access the internet and find pictures of stars and moons (perhaps using a search engine) to be used for their own creative representations	Computer Printer Internet access Paint program
	CD 2: Recognise and explore how sounds can be changed, sing simple songs from memory, recognise repeated sounds and sound patterns and match movements to music	• Look for songs and rhymes linked to the stars and moons theme on audio cassettes and CDs, CD-ROMs and the internet • Sing along and move to the selected rhymes and songs • Use CD-ROMs and internet websites to explore making and matching sounds on the theme of 'Night Time'	Computer Internet access Cassette player and audio cassettes CD player and music CDs Music software
	CD 3: Use their imagination in art and design, music, dance, imaginative and role-play and stories	• Using the above activities as a starting point, children can use their imagination to create pictures, stories and music	Computer Internet access Cassette player and audio cassettes CD player and music CDs Music software Paint program
	CD 4: Express and communicate their ideas, thoughts and feelings by using a widening range of materials, suitable tools, imaginative and role play, movement, designing and making, and a variety of songs and musical instruments	• Use a cassette recorder to record their own compositions of 'star' music • Use a video camera to record their own dance to accompany the 'star' music • Produce a class story or poem generated from the children's ideas and illustrated by pictures completed earlier using the computer	Computer Cassette player and audio cassettes CD player and music CDs

SHORT-TERM PLAN

Focus	'Stars and Moons'
Main area of learning	Creative Development
Learning objectives	CD 1: Explore colour, texture, shape, form and space in two or three dimensions
Prior learning	• Children will have explored the theme using a variety of media in the 'art area' • Children should be quite competent with the mouse • Through child-initiated activities they will be familiar with some of the features of a painting package • Children will have shared stories and rhymes linked to the theme
Activities	• Introduce the children to the idea of creating pictures using the computer • Practitioner will need to model some of the facilities of the paint software (e.g. line, shape, fill, etc.) • Children will be encouraged to create their own pictures based on the theme • Children save and print their work
Resources	• Computer • Printer • Painting software
Adult role	• Modelling the software initially • Supporting children in planning, modifying and evaluating their picture • Supporting them in using various features of the program confidently by building on existing skills and knowledge
ICT skills to be developed	• Using the different features of the painting program • Saving their work • Printing their work
Assessment opportunities	• What tools can the child use in the painting program? • Can the child save his or her work? • Can the child print his or her work?
Follow-up activities	• Use the printed pictures as illustrations to support further creative representations • Explore the internet for other pictures by real artists and by other children on the theme • Use these pictures as a basis for critical discussion or to use in their own artwork
Links with other areas of learning	CLL 2: Use talk to organise, sequence and clarify thinking and ideas PD 2: Use small equipment

10 Resources for ICT in the Foundation Stage

This chapter is designed to give you some pointers when searching for ICT-related resources for use in the Foundation Stage setting. We will begin by suggesting a number of websites of professional use to the practitioner. Most modern-day teachers will be aware that all that glitters is not gold as far as the internet is concerned but there are some nuggets to be found.

Websites for use by practitioners

There is a plethora of sites out there on the web offering the Early Years practitioner a wealth of advice, information and resources. The sites listed, and briefly reviewed, below are just some of our favourites. They will mostly be of use, professionally speaking, to the teacher although some may contain pages suitable for use by the children. Bear in mind that things change quickly on the net and web addresses in particular. They were correct at the time of going to press.

Learning with ICT at the Foundation Stage
http://vtc.ngfl.gov.uk/docserver.php?docid=2666
This is where the BECTa and VTC websites come together. This particular section contains a document mapping how ICT can support the Early Learning Goals in all six areas of learning, another outlining the development of information handling skills in the Foundation Stage and (best of all) no less than 19 detailed lesson plans applying ICT to all the areas of learning. A resource not to be missed!

Foundation Stage education and ICT
www.becta.org.uk/technology/infosheets/index.html
This information sheet gives a good overview of what should be going on, ICT-wise, in the Foundation Stage. The document is available in 'print friendly' version. There are many other useful information sheets to be found at the 'Information Sheets' home page including *Keyboard Skills in Schools*, *Acceptable Use of the Internet* and *Health and Safety: The Safe Use of ICT in Schools*.

Using ICT to support the Early Learning Goals
www.ictadvice.org.uk/
BECTa's recently launched ICT Advice site is a superb resource for all teachers, not just Foundation Stage practitioners. However, the latter will find it very enlightening if they take a look in the 'Ask an Expert' archive and locate the section entitled *Using ICT to Support the Early Learning Goals*. Here experts answer all sorts of questions regarding ICT issues, the type of questions that readers themselves would have asked. This site also offers practitioners the opportunity to join e-mail forums where they can 'talk' to other educators. The 'Foundation

Forum' is for practitioners who wish to share good practice with regard to ICT and non-ICT issues. The 'New2Computers' forum is for those practitioners who need support in getting to grips with ICT in general. There are many others – an SEN e-mailing list and a forum for ICT co-ordinators, for example. Belonging to this sort of group confirms that you are not alone in having your problems and the adage 'It's good to talk' rings true.

ICT training for teachers (TALENT)
http://ecs.lewisham.gov.uk/talent/pricor/foundation.html
A comprehensive local-authority website offering ICT activities for children in the Foundation Stage, as well as lots of resources (including plans and worksheets) for the practitioner. A list of suitable software is also given.

ICT in the Foundation Stage (Kent NGfL)
www.kented.org.uk/ngfl/foundation/index.html
Another excellent local-authority website packed with goodies! Linda Shaw discusses ICT in the Early Years. There are ideas, activities and guidance galore. The 'Infant Explorer' and 'Numeracy Explorer' sections of the site are certainly well worth exploring! Lots of ready-made files are to be found for use with *My World 3*, *Clicker 4* and the child-friendly word-processor *Textease* (Softease).

Parents' Articles: Early Learning Goals
www.bbc.co.uk/cbeebies/grownups/articles/earlylearninggoals/index.shtml
Websites for parents can be useful for the teacher too. This BBC website describes the six areas of learning and goes on to suggest *Cbeebie* websites suitable for use when developing skills in each one.

Parents Information Network (PIN)
www.pin.org.uk/
This site has a large searchable database of website and software evaluations. It could be just what you need to help you come to a decision about purchasing a certain piece of software. Alternatively, if you are looking for a CD-ROM or website to help deliver a given topic in a given area of learning this resource could be invaluable.

Other software review websites include the *BECTa Educational Software Database* (BESD) (**besd.becta.org.uk/**) and *Teachers Evaluating Educational Multimedia* (TEEM) (**www.teem.org.uk/**). We would urge practitioners to make full use of these.

ICT in Foundation Years
www.hitchams.suffolk.sch.uk/foundation/
Some school websites just cannot be ignored and the Sir Robert Hitcham Primary School website is one such example. Their section on ICT in the Foundation Stage is a must for all practitioners. The knowledgeable staff offer advice on all aspects of ICT including hardware and software reviews, using ICT in role play and in all six areas of learning. Don't miss their *Foundation ICT Top Tips*, and the

ICT Progression page makes a useful scheme of work.

Teach with ICT
www.camelsdale.w-sussex.sch.uk/default.asp
The Camelsdale First School website is full of superb resources for the Early Years practitioner. Veronica Carter, the Foundation Stage co-ordinator, has written useful articles on using *Powerpoint*, word processors and e-mail in Reception. She and other members of staff have created many *PowerPoint* presentations to be used as teaching tools in literacy and numeracy lessons. Teachers are finally coming to see the flexibility and usefulness of this software package. We would urge practitioners to jump on this bandwagon! Download some of these presentations and be inspired.

Teacher Resource Exchange (TRE)
http://tre.ngfl.gov.uk/
This site is excellent if you are looking for a specific kind of resource on a specific topic. You don't have to register but it is well worth doing so as you can then comment on the resources and actually contribute your own. The TRE is *designed to help teachers develop and share ideas for activities and resources* and includes worksheets, lesson plans and files for use with various popular programs such as *Clicker 4*, *My World 3* and *PowerPoint*.

Big Books (MAPE)
www.mape.org.uk/kids/bigbooks/index.htm
This is a wonderful resource for online 'big books'. Titles include *Muddy Time*, *Where Do Hedgehogs Go?* and the narrated *Little Red Engine*. The great thing about them (apart from being free!) is that they don't have to be viewed online. They can be downloaded to your hard disk and run from there. These could be invaluable during the Reception literacy hour.

Roamer resources
www.valiant-technology.com/
This site is a must if you have a *Roamer* in your Early Years setting. Here at the manufacturer's website you can browse a catalogue of *Roamer* accessories that you can purchase – mats for numeracy and literacy, work cards, jackets, pen packs, a poster, a video and much more. If the budget won't stretch to this then just download the extensive range of free resources. The booklet entitled *Using Roamer with the Under 5s* is particularly useful for Foundation Stage practitioners.

Pixie and Pip resources
www.swallow.co.uk/
If your programmable toy happens to be a *Pixie* (or possibly a *Pip*) then try the manufacturer's website for resources. Here you can see a catalogue of accessories, for example *Pixie* grids and playmats. There are also instructions on how to make your own. Don't miss the 'Foundation Pixie Applications' – 16 sequential activities with

photographs, diagrams and explanatory notes. For those ready to make the leap to controlling a screen turtle *Pixie Simulator* software is available. This program uses the same interface as the *Pixie* itself in the same way as *RoamerWorld* mirrors the *Roamer*.

Curriculum Online
www.curriculumonline.gov.uk/
It may have been a little late but *Curriculum Online* was finally launched by Charles Clarke, the Secretary of State for Education, in January 2003. Schools have been allocated a certain amount of E-Learning Credits (eLCs) and this portal is where practitioners can spend theirs. This means they will be able to 'purchase' many of the resources mentioned in this book. These resources include lesson plans, software, CD-ROMs, interactive videos, assessment materials, and online content and services. *Curriculum Online* is going to be a daily part of teaching in the coming years, so get used to it and see what it's got to offer the Foundation Stage.

QCA – Foundation Stage
www.qca.org.uk/ca/foundation/
This helpful website offers information about all aspects of the Foundation Stage. Here you can download the entire Foundation Stage guidance and the document *Planning for Learning in the Foundation Stage*. Also, the *Foundation Stage Profile* handbook is available for download. This replaced statutory Baseline Assessment in September 2002. There's a useful FAQ section on the curriculum and assessment.

Other useful websites

ICT in pre-school (NGfL Scotland)
www.ngflscotland.gov.uk/earlyyears/ictinpreschool.asp

National Association of Advisers for Computers in Education (NAACE)
www.naace.org/

Early Years Ideas
www.teachingideas.co.uk/earlyyears/contents.htm

ICT ideas – Early Years
www.hants.gov.uk/school/ranvilles/ranvilles2/eymenu.html

Software suggestions to support the ELGs and 'Stepping Stones'
www.ict.oxon-lea.gov.uk/software_foundation_main.html

Early Years development and childcare (DfES)
www.dfes.gov.uk/eydcp/

Preschool Learning Alliance
www.pre-school.org.uk

Nursery World
www.nursery-world.co.uk/

Websites for Foundation Stage children

As well as being a wonderful repository of resources for the practitioner, the web now has an abundance of sites, especially constructed with young children in mind, vying for their (and your) attention. Of course, this is actually another useful resource for practitioners to dip into and we thoroughly recommend the following charming websites as being more than appropriate to use with Foundation Stage children. We have categorised them according to the areas of learning but, in truth, many cover more than just one area.

Knowledge and Understanding of the World

The Swan Story
www.naturegrid.org.uk/infant/swan/bksw.html
This is part of the *Infant Explorer* site. Reception children can use this 'big book' to find out about swans, cygnets, nests and eggs. They can complete the quiz afterwards if they so wish.

BGfL Early Years Activity Centre
www.bgfl.org/bgfl/primary/ey/index.htm
Click on the 'Investigating' button to access the online activities designed to address the Knowledge and Understanding of the World area of learning. Choose from *Tidy the Classroom, Today is...* and *Young Animals*. Most areas of learning are addressed on this lovely site.

DynaMo's History
www.bbc.co.uk/education/dynamo/history/index.shtml
A marvellous BBC Education site. Various entertaining, animated, history-based activities to enchant the children.

F9-Kids
http://kids.f9.net.uk/index2.html
An excellent site full of engaging activities including information about the planets.

Children's Atlas
www.childrensatlas.com/
An online interactive atlas. Perhaps only suitable for older, more able Early Years children but any child curious about maps should find this interesting and informative.

Communication, Language and Literacy

Tiger Aki
www.asiabigtime.com/storybooks/aki_menu.html
Animated storybooks and games. The aim of the site is to help children to develop their *reading and vocabulary learning skills and enjoy computer experience by using a computer mouse*. It is particularly aimed at the preschool age group.

Words and Pictures
www.bbc.co.uk/education/wordsandpictures/
A typically wonderful BBC site to complement the school TV programme of the same name. Perhaps for older or more able Early Years children, it focuses on phonics with activities about consonant–vowel–consonant words, consonant clusters, long vowel sounds and high-frequency words. Don't miss the excellent animated poems!

Fimbles Comfy Corner
www.bbc.co.uk/cbeebies/fimbles/comfycorner/index.shtml
A selection of online talking stories – the quality doesn't get much better than this! The *Fimbles* site has much more to offer (again, not a surprise given that it is a BBC site) if you have the time to take a look around.

The Hoobs
www.channel4.com/learning/microsites/H/hoobs/activities/archive.cfm
Lots of online activities featuring the loveable TV characters addressing literacy (and numeracy) at the Foundation Stage that children will love. Teachers will like the fact that printable worksheets (listed under the six areas of learning) are available for downloading.

Ladybird
www.ladybird.co.uk/
The popular children's book publisher's site. The 'Storytime', 'Fun and Games' and 'Topsy and Tim' sections are full of entertaining and educational reading activities. Good use is made of sound and animation.

The Little Animals Activity Centre
www.bbc.co.uk/education/laac/
Another amazing BBC site which helps to develop many skills including those of literacy. Of particular interest are Digby Mole's word games (word matching, rhyming words and first letters) and Storybear's animated tales with sound.

Tweenies
www.bbc.co.uk/education/tweenies/index.shtml
A site that complements the popular TV programme for young children. Visit 'Story Time' to hear traditional tales and stories about the Tweenie characters.

Bob the Builder
www.hitentertainment.com/bobthebuilder/
Another site linked to a TV series for young children. Many online activities are available but in terms of literacy skills Mrs Percival's spelling lessons will be of most interest.

Planet Wobble
www.planetwobble.com

If you use this scheme for early readers, and also the associated software, you may like to take the children to the *Planet Wobble* website. Why? Well, the children can e-mail their favourite character using an online form and get a reply! Their e-mail may even be highlighted on the site.

Mathematical Development

Numbertime
www.bbc.co.uk/education/numbertime/
An excellent site linked to the BBC school TV programme of the same name. A number of interactive games are on offer that develop skills of adding, number recognition and matching, ordering and counting.

Compare It!
http://hbogucki.staffnet.com/aemes/apps/compare/compare.htm
Not a great site for 'whistles and bells' but an infinitely customisable site for the teacher of older Early Years children who wants to give his or her class practice in such concepts as 'less than', 'more than' or 'equal to'. Words, pictures and/or symbols can be used.

Learning Planet: Preschool Games
www.learningplanet.com/kids1.htm
Excellent online games addressing such skills as number recognition, counting and ordering. American but very usable.

Rabbits in Teletubbyland
www.bbc.co.uk/cbeebies/teletubbies/
Count the rabbits in 'Laa-Laa's Book' or play the 'More than One' game. Other areas of learning catered for.

Loose Change Shopping Game
www.oup.co.uk/oxed/primary/funzone/funzone.html/omzshopping.html/
Drag the coins out of the purse and drop them into the slot. The aim is make the coins add up to the price tag on the object. For older, more able Early Years children.

Personal, Social and Emotional Development, Physical Development and Creative Development

Tweenies Song Time
www.bbc.co.uk/cbeebies/tweenies/songtime/index.shtml
Lots of children's favourite songs to sing along to. You can also print out the words.

LittleKids Stories
www.bbc.co.uk/cbeebies/stories/
Children can read (or listen to) some of their favourite stories such as *Cinderella* or *Jack and the beanstalk*. The stories all have a positive outcome.

Crayola Kids
www.crayola.com/kids/index.cfm
Lots of colouring and art activities here. Some are online activities but there are plenty of printable materials too.

Welltown
www.welltown.gov.uk/menu.htm
Children can visit the health centre, the house, the school or the park on the government's hygiene, health and safety site for young children.

Toddler Town
www.education.com/jumpstart/toddlertown/
A superb place to develop hand–eye co-ordination, mouse and keyboard skills through playing interactive games such as 'Puzzle Pals' and 'Tub Time'.

CBeebies
www.bbc.co.uk/cbeebies/
This huge site offers a wealth of online (and printable) activities for young children most of which are hosted by children's TV favourites. 'Artbox' is the best online suite of art-related activities we have seen. 'Music Game' and 'Tikkabilla Jive' are just some of the musical activities available whilst 'Clic-a-pic' brings on those all-important mouse skills.

ICT Resources
http://ngfl.northumberland.gov.uk/ict/default.htm
This local-authority website has some great activities to develop 'Early Mouse Skills'. Don't forget to peruse the 'Simple Control' exercises where the little red ship must be guided to the lighthouse.

Early Birds Music
www.earlybirdsmusic.com/
A great source of original action songs for the Early Years. Check out 'Spaceman Sid Songs' but make sure you have *RealOne Player* installed. There are also MP3 files available.

ICT in the Foundation Stage
www.edu.dudley.gov.uk/foundation/index2.htm
A local-authority site with links to online activities for all areas of learning. A quick and handy resource.

CD-ROMs for Foundation Stage children

The use of CD-ROMs is stressed a great deal in the guidance and we recommend building up a library of titles. A 'try before you buy' policy is wise here. All too often people get excited by the blinding multimedia dazzle of these disks and these blur their judgement. A hasty purchase can soon lead to disenchantment as they realise that a title offers a lot of 'flash' but little substance. Teachers have been judging the educational value of resources for years and CD-ROMs are no different. Take the time to 'test drive' a title you are thinking of purchasing and make a judgement as to its worth in the classroom.

There is a bewildering choice out there in the education market place. Below we mention, and briefly review, some of our particular favourites.

Knowledge and Understanding of the World
The Jolly Postman (Dorling Kindersley) – based on the original books by Janet and Allan Ahlberg. This title develops literacy and numeracy skills, and introduces children to geography and design. For older, more able children.

Fourways Farm – Autumn (Channel 4) – linked to the popular schools TV programme. It allows children to explore scientific concepts such as materials, plants and sound through video and interactive tasks. The growth of pupils' scientific vocabulary is encouraged, as is their understanding of the concepts involved.

Play and Learn Science and Experiments (Dorling Kindersley) – provides a safe environment for younger Early Years children to experiment and discover such concepts as magnetism, gravity, light and colour.

Let's Go with Katy (SCET) – modules 1–3 will be of most interest to Early Years practitioners. This lovable character introduces the concepts of left, right, orientation and bearings.

Become a History Explorer (Dorling Kindersley) – for older, more able children. They can travel back in time to exciting events and important times in history and find out all about them.

Design and Technology (Widget Software) – lots of *My World* screens involving D&T activities on various topics including food, fashion and buildings.

Teddy Bears' Picnic (Sherston) – a delightful new title for 4–6-year-olds that develops literacy and numeracy concepts whilst consolidating ICT skills. All this is done within the context of the familiar theme of the teddy bears' picnic. Lovely graphics, animations and narration.

Communication, Language and Literacy
Read and Write with Rat-a-tat-tat (Channel 4) – designed to accompany the school television programme. It has a phonic approach to reading and writing focusing on letter formation and spelling to encourage young children to develop handwriting and reading skills.

Bailey's Book House (Iona) – interactive activities aid the child in learning letter names and sounds. Also, rhyming words, the meaning of words and how words relate to pictures are covered.

Learning Ladder: Preschool (Dorling Kindersley) – structured educational games. Reading skills (the alphabet, phonics, first words) and writing skills (handwriting, making words) are highlighted (maths skills included also).

Talking Animated Alphabet (Sherston) – uses sound, graphics and animation to good effect to teach visual and aural discrimination and letter recognition. Letters 'morph' into objects with the same initial sound. This gives young children a powerful visual and aural link between the letter shape and sound.

Rhyme and Analogy (Sherston) – a suite of activities that aid the development of phonological skills. The activities are graded to increase steadily the young child's knowledge of rhyme, letters and sounds.

Words and Pictures Alphabet (Longman Logotron) – designed to accompany the school television series but can be used independently of it. This package is for older, more advanced Early Years children and focuses on higher-level language skills.

Starspell 2001 (Fisher-Marriot) – a popular spelling program for Reception children in the literacy hour. Lists of words on many topics are given but teachers can enter their own to suit the age and ability of the child and the context. Sound and picture clues are given to assist development of spelling skills. The package uses the 'look-cover-write-check' approach to spelling.

My First Dictionary (Dorling Kindersley) – an excellent first dictionary for young children who need to find out how words are spelt and their meanings. The program reinforces knowledge of alphabetical order and offers a variety of word games. Reading and spelling skills will be enhanced.

Mathematical Development

Millie's Math House (Iona) – uses music, sound effects, speech and animation to aid the development of such things as number recognition, shapes, sequences and the concept of size.

My First CD-ROM: Number (Dorling Kindersley) – activities to promote counting and sorting introduced by White Bear and Little Penguin. This numeracy package is especially for 3–5-year-olds. Older, more able Early Years children can move on to the next program in the series, *Bear and Penguin's Big Maths Adventure* where the same characters foster the skills of adding and subtracting.

123-CD (Sherston) – activities to promote the learning of early number skills. 'Number Rhymes', 'Number Names' and 'How Many?' are just some of the useful games to play.

Number Train (Sherston) – practice in mental mathematics. Ordering numbers, odd and even numbers, counting in twos, simple addition and subtraction are among the activities children can opt for. Engaging characters and helpful speech assist the learner. A version of this program is available on the DfEE's CD-ROM *Using*

ICT to Support Mathematics in Schools.

Reader Rabbit Maths: 4–6 (Learning Company) – activities to develop skills in counting, number patterns, simple addition and subtraction. Also useful for practice of matching numbers to sets of objects and recognising equal and unequal sums.

Numbertime: Time (Longman Logotron) – introduces young children to the notion of time in a very gentle way. Colourful animations and entertaining sounds take them through such concepts as sequencing events, time of day, time of year and the clock face.

Percy's Money Box (Neptune) – an easy introduction to money. Skills developed include identifying coins and recognising amounts of money. The children have to buy items from a shop using the correct coins and working out the required change.

Personal, Social and Emotional Development, Physical Development and Creative Development

Bananas in Pyjamas (Dorling Kindersley) – includes lots of interactive games, children's songs and nursery rhymes.

Tiny Draw Plus (Topologika) – a simple art package especially for younger children with all the usual tools.

Compose World Junior (ESP) – a music program where pictures represent phrases of music. These phrases build into compositions that can be played in various styles.

Choices, Choices Series (Tom Snyder) – these programs develop the knowledge, skills and understanding needed to make the right choices in a variety of situations at school. Decent-quality graphics and sound effects hold the attention of the children as they develop their social responsibility.

Tizzy's Toybox (Sherston) – a cross-curricular package for preschool children. Early literacy and numeracy skills are developed by the use of the games on this disk, as well as colour recognition and mouse skills.

The essential software kit for the Foundation Stage

The CD-ROMs mentioned above are fine examples of the kind of multimedia extravaganzas available today. Having some of these titles to hand in your Early Years setting will be no bad thing. But what about the 'bread and butter' software needed by Foundation Stage practitioners to deliver a broad and balanced ICT experience? These are purely our recommendations – no doubt you will have your own favourites:

- *Clicker 4*
- *Textease*
- *My World 3*

- *Counter for Windows*
- *Kidpix Studio*
- *Compose World Junior*
- *FlexiTREE*
- *Oxford Reading Tree*
- *Using ICT to Support Mathematics in the Primary School*
- *Infant Video Toolbox*
- *Internet Explorer (web browser)*

Free software for the Foundation Stage

Making these recommendations about desirable software packages and marvellous multimedia CD-ROMs is all very well but what if your Early Years setting is short of the necessary funds to purchase them? Never fear! Help is at hand in the form of *freeware* downloadable from the internet. As these programs are free you might be forgiven for thinking that they lack quality and, more importantly, any educational value. However, to dismiss them out of hand would, in our opinion, be a mistake. Below we direct you to some specific programs and to some to sites where many useful (very useful!) packages can be downloaded gratis.

Facetoon
www.hants.gov.uk/school/ranvilles/ranvilles2/ict17.html
This eye-catching program develops mouse skills through giving a face its features. It's a 'fuzzy felt' package that focuses on the essential skill of dragging and dropping.

Sebran's ABC
www.aw.nu/Sebran/index_eng.asp
This suite of 12 literacy and numeracy programs will impress you we are sure. Colourful graphics and cheerful music accompany the activities. A great 'freebie'!

Music Games
www.inclusive.co.uk/downloads/downloads.shtml#musicgames
On Inclusive Technology's 'Free Downloads' page you will find this musical gem. Very useful in the creative development area of learning.

SENSwitcher
www.northerngrid.org/sen/intro.htm
According to the developers of this free program, *SENSwitcher is a suite of programs designed to help teach early ICT skills to people with profound and multiple learning difficulties, those who need to develop skills with assistive input devices and very young children new to*

computers. We feel there's no more to be said.

Literacy Time – Free Software
curriculum.becta.org.uk/literacy/resources/software/free_software.html
The Literacy Time website, in our opinion, is a must for all teachers anyway but the free software page has some interesting downloads on offer including *Hangman Gold* and links to other freeware sites.

Grey Olltwit's Freeware
www.adders.org/freeware/
There are lots of educational programs to be found here, for use in several areas of learning, including *Loose Change*, *Musical Pairs* and *Counting Frame* to name but a few.

Kids Freeware
http://kidsfreeware.com/
Beware when visiting this site! There are so many wonderful free programs here that before you know it you will have spent hours at the keyboard when you could be having a life! Seriously, this site has educational packages suitable for use in all areas of learning and all abilities. Put some time aside to have a good browse.

Owl & Mouse educational software
www.yourchildlearns.com/owlmouse.htm
This site has a lot of simple literacy and reading software to offer but there are some other programs that may well catch your eye as well.

Kids Domain – downloads ages 2–5
www.kidsdomain.com/down/pc/_age2to5-index.html
This site has dozens of freely downloadable programs under various headings. These include 'Art and Creativity', 'Language', 'Maths' and 'Music'.

Riverdeep – free downloads
www.riverdeep.com/products/downloads/free_downloads.jhtml
There are some nice programs for the Early Years (PreK) to be found here, especially with regard to literacy (*Letter Machine*) and numeracy (*Little, Middle & Big*).

Essential ICT equipment for the Foundation Stage

Here we list what we see as desirable ICT devices and apparatus for the Early Years setting. We realise budgets might not stretch to accommodate all these and, indeed, practitioners may not think of some of the items listed as being 'essential'. Nevertheless, the more of these that you can afford the better, as young children's chances of getting to grips with today's ICT-rich world are increased.

Computer-related hardware

- multimedia computer(s)
- large monitor
- lower-case keyboard
- small mouse
- colour printer
- speakers
- headphones
- microphones
- overlay keyboard
- scanner
- internet access (broadband)

Other ICT resources

- television
- video recorder/player
- digital camera
- video camera
- programmable toys
- cassette recorder/player
- CD/DVD player
- radio
- music keyboards
- telephones (toy and real)
- toy cash register
- calculators (with large keys)

Further reading

Books

Farr, A (2001) *ICT Activities (Early Years Activity Chest)*. Leamington Spa: Scholastic.

Farr, A (2001) *Using ICT (Skills for Early Years)*. Leamington Spa: Scholastic.

Keating, I (ed.) (2002) *Teaching Foundation Stage*. Exeter: Learning Matters.

Potter, J (2002) *PGCE Professional Workbook: Primary ICT*. Exeter: Learning Matters.

Sharp, J, Potter, J, Allen, J and Loveless, A (2000) *Primary ICT: Knowledge, Understanding and Practice*. Exeter: Learning Matters.

Siraj-Blatchford, J and Whitebread, D (2002) *Supporting ICT in the Early Years*. Milton Keynes: Open University Press.

Journals

Early Years Educator (monthly magazine that refers to ICT). London: Mark Allen Publishing.

Nursery Education (monthly magazine that refers to ICT). Leamington Spa: Scholastic.

Nursery World (weekly magazine that refers to ICT). London: TSL Education.

Ager, R. (1998) *ICT in the Primary School*. London: David Fulton.

Alliance for Childhood (2000) *Fool's Gold: A Critical Look at Computers in Childhood*. College Park, MD: Alliance for Childhood. (**www.allianceforchildhood.net/projects/computers/computers_reports.htm**)

BECTa (2000) *A Preliminary Report for the DfEE on the Relationship between ICT and Primary School Standards*. Coventry: BECTa.

BECTa (2001) *BECTa Primary Schools of the Future: Achieving Today*. Coventry: BECTa.

BECTa (2002) *ImpaCT2 Report* (www.becta.org.uk/research/impaCT2)

BESA (2002) *Information and Communication Technology in UK State Schools*. London: BESA.

Collins, J., Hammond, M. and Wellington, J. (1997) *Teaching and Learning with Multimedia*. London: Routledge.

Cook, D. and Finlayson, H. (1999) *Interactive Children, Communicative Teaching*. Buckingham: Open University Press.

DfEE (1998) *Teaching: High Status, High Standards*. London: DfEE.

DfES (2003) *ICT in Schools*. London: DfES (**www.dfes.gov.uk/ictinschools/index.shtml**).

DfES/TTA (2002) *Qualifying to Teach*. London: DfES/TTA.

Donahue, T. (2003) Pedagogical advantages of the Roamer (article available at **www.valiant-technology.com**).

Fine, C. and Thornbury, M.L. (1998) Control and literacy. *MAPE Magazine*.

Grenier, J. and Thornbury, M.L. (2001) Adults and children at the computer in the nursery, in Wake, B. (2001) *Beyond the School Gate*. Northampton: Castlefield.

Hall, E. and Higgins, S. (2002) Embedding Computer Technology in Developmentally Appropriate Practice: Engaging with Early Years Professionals' Beliefs and Values. *Information Technology in Childhood Education*, Vol. 2002, issue 1, pp 293–312. Norfolk, USA: AACE.

Hoare, S. (2002) Sticky fingers. *Guardian*, 8 January.

Loveless, A. (1995) *The Role of IT: Practical Issues for the Primary Teacher*. London: Cassell.

Medwell, J. (1996) Talking books and reading. *Reading*, April: 416.

Mills, C. and Mills, D. (1997) *Britain's Early Years Disaster* (script for a Channel 4 television programme). London: Mills Production.

OFSTED (2002) *ICT in Schools: Effect of Government Initiatives*. London: OFSTED.

Pange, J. and Kontozisis, D. (2001) Introducing Computers to Kindergarten Children based on Vygotsky's Theory about Socio-cultural Learning: the Greek perspective. *Information Technology in Childhood Education*, Vol. 2001, issue 1, pp 193–202.

Norfolk, USA: AACE.

Potter, J. (2002) *PGCE Professional Workbook: Primary ICT*. Exeter: Learning Matters.

QCA/DfEE (2000) *Curriculum Guidance for the Foundation Stage*. London: QCA/DfEE.

Siraj-Blatchford, J. and Siraj-Blatchford, I. (2002) *Kidsmart: The Phase 1 UK Evaluation 2000–2001 Final Project Report*. (**www.ioe.ac.uk/cdl/datec/finawebCopy.pdf**)

Scrimshaw, P. in Somekh, B. and Davis, N. (eds) (1997) *Using IT Effectively in Teaching and Learning*. London: Routledge.

Smith, H. (1999) *Opportunities for Information and Communication Technology in the Primary School*. Stoke-on-Trent: Trentham Books.

Smithers, R. (2001) Survey reveals teachers' anxiety over digital divide. *Guardian*, 18 October.

University of Newcastle (1999) *Ways forward with ICT*. Newcastle: University of Newcastle.

Weeks, B. (2000) What are the most efficient teaching strategies for information technology in the Early Years? *MAPE Magazine*, 3.

Index